First printing: July 2020
Third printing: March 2022

Master Books® is a division of the
New Leaf Publishing Group, Inc.

ISBN: 978-1-68344-193-9
ISBN: 978-1-61458-753-8 (digital)
Library of Congress Number: 2020936608

Cover and Interior design: Diana Bogardus

Unless otherwise noted, Scripture quotations are from the English Standard Version (ESV) of the Bible

Please consider requesting that a copy of this volume be purchased by your local library system.

Printed in China

Master Books®
A Division of New Leaf Publishing Group
www.masterbooks.com

Please visit our website for other great titles:
www.masterbooks.com

ABOUT THE AUTHOR

Craig Froman was born in California (in the West), then moved to Missouri (in the Midwest), and now he lives with his precious wife and kids in Arkansas (in the South). The summer before he started 6th grade, his family loaded up in a camper and drove for six weeks around the United States, traveling through 31 states and exploring so many wonders of God's world. He's since traveled to 40 of the 50 states, including Hawaii, and loves all the places he's been able to see with his own eyes. Now he is the assistant editor at New Leaf Publishing Group and author of *Passport to the World* and *Children's Atlas of God's World*. He has a Bachelor of Arts in business administration and a master's degree in education.

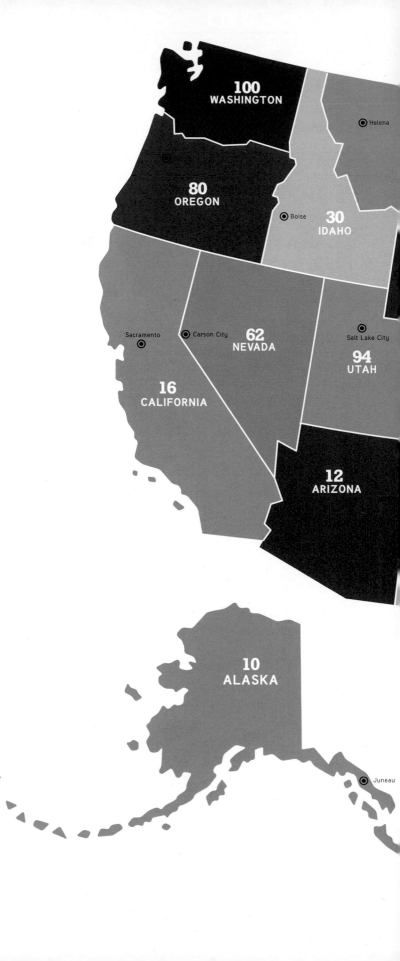

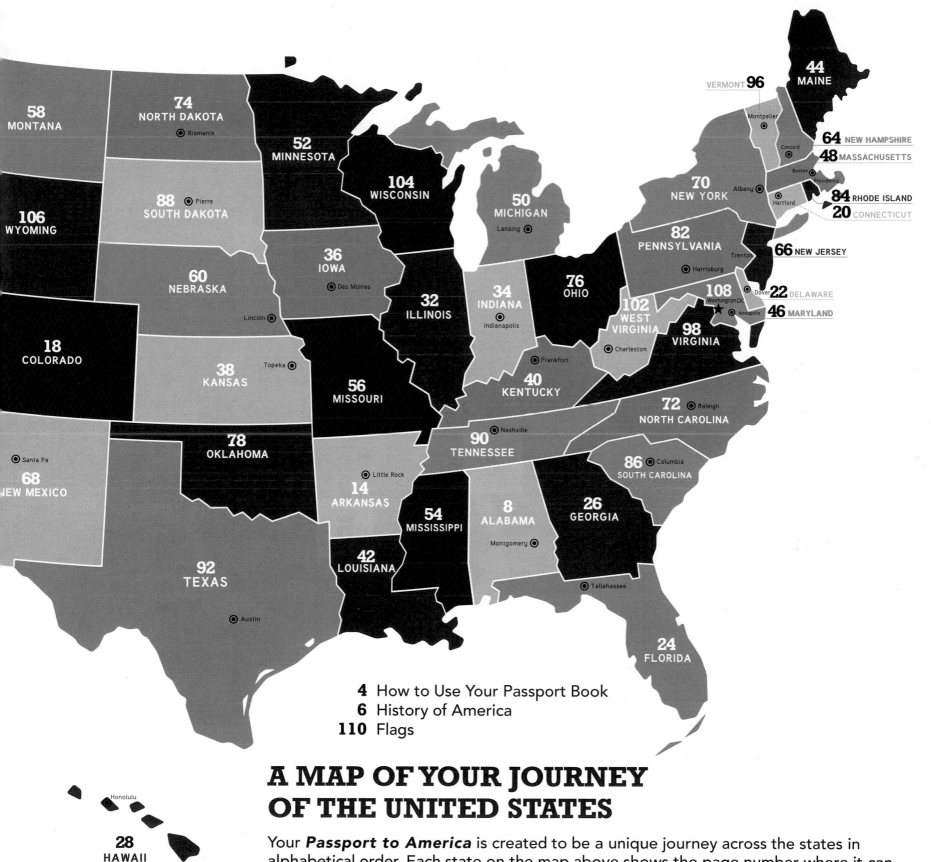

58 MONTANA

74 NORTH DAKOTA
◉ Bismarck

52 MINNESOTA

104 WISCONSIN

50 MICHIGAN
Lansing ◉

44 MAINE

VERMONT **96**
Montpelier ◉

64 NEW HAMPSHIRE
Concord ◉

48 MASSACHUSETTS
Boston ◉
Providence ◉

70 NEW YORK
Albany ◉

84 RHODE ISLAND
Hartford ◉

20 CONNECTICUT

106 WYOMING

88 SOUTH DAKOTA
◉ Pierre

36 IOWA
◉ Des Moines

82 PENNSYLVANIA
Trenton ◉

66 NEW JERSEY
◉ Harrisburg

18 COLORADO

60 NEBRASKA
Lincoln ◉

32 ILLINOIS

34 INDIANA
◉ Indianapolis

76 OHIO

102 WEST VIRGINIA
◉ Charleston

108
Washington DC ★
◉ Annapolis

22 DELAWARE
◉ Dover

46 MARYLAND

98 VIRGINIA

38 KANSAS
Topeka ◉

56 MISSOURI

40 KENTUCKY
◉ Frankfort

72 NORTH CAROLINA
◉ Raleigh

68 NEW MEXICO
Santa Fe ◉

78 OKLAHOMA

14 ARKANSAS
◉ Little Rock

90 TENNESSEE
◉ Nashville

86 SOUTH CAROLINA
◉ Columbia

54 MISSISSIPPI

8 ALABAMA
Montgomery ◉

26 GEORGIA

92 TEXAS
◉ Austin

42 LOUISIANA

24 FLORIDA
◉ Tallahassee

A MAP OF YOUR JOURNEY OF THE UNITED STATES

Your **Passport to America** is created to be a unique journey across the states in alphabetical order. Each state on the map above shows the page number where it can be found. Enjoy!

Honolulu

28 HAWAII

HOW TO USE YOUR PASSPORT BOOK ★ ★ ★ ★ ★

Welcome to the start of an incredible journey across the United States! Your book is set up in alphabetical order by the 50 states. You will cross over mountains, rivers, and oceans, all the while in the comfort of your own living room, car, or backyard tent!

1 **State:** This is the name of the specific state you are visiting. Most of the facts listed will relate to the state, which includes history and God's natural wonders there. You will also learn about cultural and traditional customs.

2 **State flag:** Here you will find information on the flag of the state you are visiting. This will include the reasoning behind the colors and the symbols, and sometimes who came up with the design itself!

3 **State stats:** Here you can quickly find out details about the state, which includes a map, the capital, state postal abbreviation, U.S. Census Bureau region, and size of the state in square miles. Find the highlighted state and its capital city, as well as where it is in relation to neighboring states, lakes, or oceans.

4 **State motto:** Read the phrase that represents the slogan or proverb from that particular state.

5 **Greeting from a friend:** Read a welcome from a friend to learn more about the state, as well as to see how the name of the state came to be.

6 **State stamp:** This is a special stamp with images that represent the state and the people there.

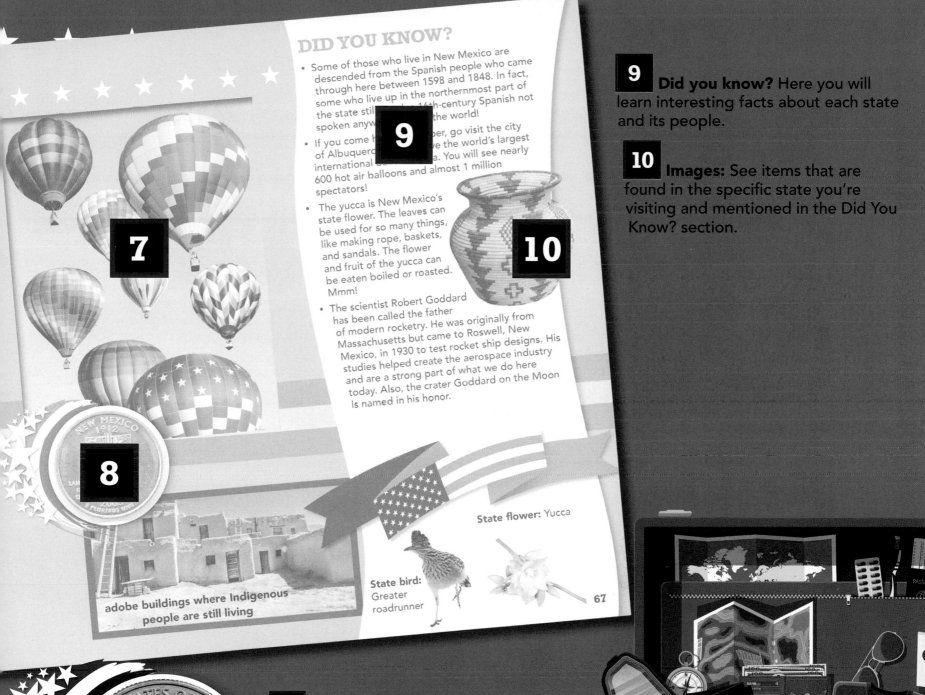

DID YOU KNOW?

- Some of those who live in New Mexico are descended from the Spanish people who came through here between 1598 and 1848. In fact, some who live up in the northernmost part of the state still speak a 16th-century Spanish not spoken anywhere in the world!

- If you come here in October, go visit the city of Albuquerque to see the world's largest international balloon fiesta. You will see nearly 600 hot air balloons and almost 1 million spectators!

- The yucca is New Mexico's state flower. The leaves can be used for so many things, like making rope, baskets, and sandals. The flower and fruit of the yucca can be eaten boiled or roasted. Mmm!

- The scientist Robert Goddard has been called the father of modern rocketry. He was originally from Massachusetts but came to Roswell, New Mexico, in 1930 to test rocket ship designs. His studies helped create the aerospace industry and are a strong part of what we do here today. Also, the crater Goddard on the Moon is named in his honor.

State flower: Yucca

State bird: Greater roadrunner

adobe buildings where Indigenous people are still living

67

9 **Did you know?** Here you will learn interesting facts about each state and its people.

10 **Images:** See items that are found in the specific state you're visiting and mentioned in the Did You Know? section.

7 **Picture:** This picture shows a little something interesting about the state, its cities, mountains, lakes, and more.

8 **State quarters:** See images of the state's special quarters.

5

HISTORY OF AMERICA ★ ★ ★

WHERE THE AMERICAN STORY BEGINS . . .

God created the lands that we call America, or the United States, back when He created the world, as recorded in the first chapters of Genesis. There were no people here at that time. The first people would have started their journey here a little over 4,000 years ago. Everyone was living on a plain in Shinar, an area of the Middle East. God wanted them to fill the earth, but they wanted to stay there, desiring to work together to build a tower to show how great they were. This is the Tower of Babel, the account of which you can find in Genesis 11:1–9.

THE PEOPLE BEGIN THEIR JOURNEY

According to the historical account in Genesis, the Lord altered the languages of the people, and they went off into the world with those who spoke the same language they did.

It is interesting how many cultures refer to the ancient account of the tower. There is a Sumerian legend, a story from Mexico, an account passed down from the native people of Arizona, as well as stories from Nepal, Myanmar, Tanzania, and more. The first people to step onto what is now American soil would have come across an ice bridge created during the Ice Age between what is now the Asian continent and Alaska.

THE NATIVE PEOPLES

The people walking to North America didn't all come at once. They came in waves — some staying in the colder northern areas while others moved farther south, finally filling what is now the major land area of the United States, as well as Central and South America. By the time the first Europeans sailed across the Atlantic — these being the Norse people as far back as A.D. 1001 — the Native Americans were living throughout all the major areas of North and South America. These first settlers left a legacy of language, and it's interesting that over 170 native languages are still spoken in the United States. So, thousands of years ago, the first movement of what are often called immigrants began. Immigrants leave their land or country and go to live in another land. Many more waves of people would come later — by foot, by ship, by car, by bus, and by plane.

THE NEW WAVES OF IMMIGRANTS

The next Europeans to travel to North and South America came from Spain, England, and Portugal. The most famous of these expeditions was led by Christopher Columbus in 1492. This Italian explorer was funded by the Spanish, seeking a shorter trade route to India. Soon the Spanish began to conquer the native people who lived on the land, and more countries began sailing across the Atlantic to establish villages and towns.

People would eventually come to America from nearly every nation on earth, which meant bringing their distinctive beliefs, languages, and customs. This has created both a wonderful mix of ideas and thoughts that can be shared and also frustration and anxiety in having to try to find common ground for so many different people. This is a good place to remember that we should always seek peace when we can. Jesus talked about being a people of peace when He said: "Blessed are the peacemakers, for they shall be called sons of God" (Matthew 5:9).

The birth of the United States began when the 13 original colonies rose up against Britain and declared their independence in 1776. These colonies became the first 13 states, and eventually, 37 more states would be added. There are also special territories of the United States. These are American Samoa, Baker Island, Guam Howland Island, Jarvis Island, Johnston Atoll, Kingman Reef, Midway Islands, Navassa Island, Northern Mariana Islands, Palmyra Atoll, Puerto Rico, Virgin Islands, and Wake Island.

Declaration

July 4, 1776

It is interesting that the United States does not have an official national language, though the majority of people do speak English. There are over 400 languages in the country that are either spoken or signed (for the Deaf). This includes Spanish, Chinese, Tagalog, French, Arabic, Russian, German, Bengali, Hebrew, and Navajo. One of the languages spoken here, American Sign Language, was created for the Deaf community.

WHERE THIS STORY WILL END

The Bible tells us that one day there will be people gathered to God from all over the world because of His love shown through His Son Jesus. The blood Jesus shed on the Cross will ransom, or save, "people for God from every tribe and language and people and nation" (Revelation 5:9). This will include people from the United States!

LET'S GO!

You normally only need a passport if you come to the United States from another country. It's not something you need as you travel from state to state. However, you can get a passport kind of stamp at every U.S. capitol building. Make sure you keep your small passport book handy as you go from state to state, and as you read each one put a state flag sticker in it from the back of the book.

ALABAMA ★ ★ ★ ★ ★ ★ ★

STATE STATS

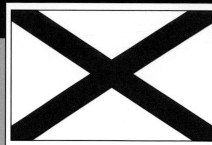

Square Miles: 52,420

Capital: Montgomery

Postal abbreviation: AL

U.S. region: The South

State motto: We dare defend our rights

The state flag is white with a red cross, created to look like the Confederate battle flag. The official name of the flag is the "crimson cross of St. Andrew's," and it can be rectangular or square.

SPECIAL FOOD
Chicken and White Barbecue Sauce

Hello friends!

We're here in the South, and our state name comes from the language of the Choctaw people and means "thicket-clearers" or "vegetation gatherers." If you come to Montgomery, you'll see our state capital building. Our capital city was named after Richard Montgomery, who was a Revolutionary War general. At 52,420 square miles, we're ranked number 30 in size out of the 50 states. Welcome to Alabama!

ALABAMA U.S.A.

★★ ALABAMA

OCT **Alabama** 17
55BC577

Middle Bay Lighthouse, Mobile, Alabama

Saturn V rocket

NASA

- The very first citywide electric trolley system in America was in Montgomery. It started up back in 1886.

- A resident of Alabama named Sequoyah created the written alphabet of the Cherokee language. This helped the Cherokee people begin to read and write in their own language.

- The airport in Birmingham opened up in 1931. Back then, a flight from Birmingham to Los Angeles took about 19 hours. Now it only takes between 6 to 7 hours!

- The Saturn V rocket was built by NASA to send people to the moon. That V in the name is for the Roman numeral five. This rocket was used in the Apollo space program during the 1960s and 1970s and was developed in Huntsville, Alabama, at NASA's Marshall Space Flight Center.

State flower: Camellia

State bird: Northern Flicker

9

ALASKA ★ ★ ★ ★ ★

STATE STATS

Square Miles: 665,384

Capital: Juneau

Postal abbreviation: AK

U.S. region: The West

State motto: North to the future

Designed by Benny Benson in 1927, who was an orphan. You see the Big Dipper on the dark blue background. The big star on the right side stands for the North Star, Polaris, and the state farthest in the north, which is Alaska.

ALASKA U.S.A NOV 3 8PM

ALASKA

SPECIAL FOOD

Alaskan king crab legs

Greetings from Alaska!

Our state name is from the native Aleut language and can mean "great land," "mainland," or "the object the sea waves break against." Our state is the largest state! The total area of the land is 665,384 square miles. We're so big that if you place a map of Alaska over the 48 lower states, it would stretch from coast to coast, and we have over 6,600 miles of coastline. Our capital city is named after a gold prospector named Joe Juneau. Hope to see you in Alaska soon!

SEP ALASKA 00 DFW 167 • The Last Frontier •

Grizzly bears hunting salmon

DID YOU KNOW?

- In 1925, the serum to help people in a horrible diphtheria epidemic in Nome was considered unsafe to use because the batch of serum there had expired. The call went out for more, but the closest place was 938 miles away in Anchorage. The only means at the time to transport the medicine quickly was by dog sled, so this "Great Race of Mercy" began with the medicine being taken by train 298 miles, then by dog sled teams, getting there in only 5½ days.

Gunnar Kaasen with Balto

- The Iditarod dog sled race was first held in 1973. It was created to honor the serum run of 1925. The average time for these sleds is between 8 and 15 days. Dog mushing is an official state sport approved by the Alaska Legislature in 1972.

- The record high temperature in Alaska occurred in 1915 when it hit 100 degrees Fahrenheit at Fort Yukon. The record low occurred in 1971 at Prospect Creek Camp. The temperature was -80 degrees Fahrenheit!

A musher heads out of Willow towards Nome, Alaska in the Iditarod

ALASKA 1959
THE GREAT LAND
2008
E PLURIBUS UNUM

State flower: Forget-me-not

State bird: Willow ptarmigan

11

ARIZONA ★ ★ ★ ★ ★ ★ ★ ★ ★

STATE STATS

Square Miles: 113,990

Capital: Phoenix

Postal abbreviation: AZ

U.S. region: The West

State motto: God enriches

The 13 stripes stand for the original 13 states. These red and yellow colors represent the colors of the Spanish conquistadors who came through Arizona in 1540. The star in the center is copper-colored and stands for Arizona's copper production. The flag was officially adopted in 1917.

SPECIAL FOOD

Chimichangas

Hi!

Our name, Arizona, is from the O'odham language and is thought to mean "young spring" or "a little spring." If you look at the map, you can find our capital city, Phoenix. Some settlers passing through the area in 1867 named it to reflect their new town rising up from the ruins of the former native civilization. A phoenix is a mythical bird that rises from ashes. At 113,990 square miles, our state is the 6th largest of the 50 states. So glad you could visit Arizona!

Praying Hands Formation near Apache Junction, Arizona

ARIZONA 15 NOV
BJV7821
GRAND CANYON STATE

DID YOU KNOW?

- The massive Grand Canyon was carved by the movement of the receding waters after the great Flood. People explore it by hiking the trails or rafting on the Colorado River down below. Another way to get to the bottom is on a mule. Mules began carrying people up and down the Canyon back in the 1890s.

- Meteor Crater is a huge hole in the ground caused by . . . you guessed it . . . a meteor striking the earth! It measures approximately 4,200 feet across and around 570 feet deep.

- In the 1830s, the original London Bridge in London, England, was built across the River Thames. Then, in 1967, they completely took it apart and relocated it to Lake Havasu, Arizona. Each block from the original bridge was numbered and brought to America so they could rebuild it right!

State flower: Blossom of the Saguaro Cactus

State bird: Cactus wren

13

ARKANSAS ★ ★ ★ ★ ★ ★ ★

STATE STATS

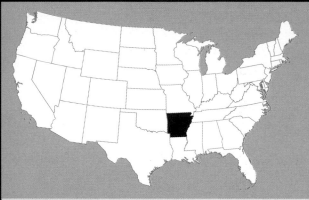

Square Miles: 53,179

Capital: Little Rock

Postal abbreviation: AR

U.S. region: The South

State motto: The people rule

The flag has the colors of red, white, and blue. The diamond shape represents the diamonds mined in the state. The 25 stars in the diamond are to remind people that Arkansas was the 25th state.

SPECIAL FOOD

Fried dill pickles

Hey Ya'll!

People from France took the name of our state from the native Kansa word *akaansa*, which basically means "people of the wind." We're here in the South, and our capital city is called Little Rock. In 1722, a French explorer named the area along the river Little Rock because there was a stone outcropping that was easy for people traveling the river to spot. The name stuck! At 53,179 square miles, we are ranked 29 out of the 50 states. Welcome to Arkansas!

Crystal Bridges Museum of American Art

514 KZE

The Natural State

DID YOU KNOW?

- Near Murfreesboro, Arkansas, you can visit the Crater of Diamonds State Park. It's the only diamond mine in the United States, and you can go into the mine and dig for diamonds or other gemstones, like agate, garnet, and jasper. You get to keep any gems you find!

- On the southwestern slope of Hot Springs Mountain flow 47 hot springs. The water has an average temperature of 143° F.

- Want to visit the World's Championship Duck Calling Contest? It's held each year in Stuttgart!

- The world's largest retail chain, Walmart, has its headquarters in the state. Alice Walton of the Walmart family founded the Crystal Bridges Museum of American Art in Bentonville. This wondrous museum was designed by Moshe Safdie, and it opened in 2011.

Small waterfall near Hot Springs, Arkansas

Various duck calls

State bird: Mockingbird

State flower: Apple blossom

STATE STATS

Square Miles: 163,696

Capital: Sacramento

Postal abbreviation: CA

U.S. region: The West

State motto: Eureka! (I have found it)

CALIFORNIA REPUBLIC

You can see why California's state flag is called the Bear Flag because there is a grizzly bear in the center. First used as early as 1846 by settlers who were revolting against the rule of Mexico, it had the bear, a red bar, and a five-pointed star. Later the words "California Republic" were added. The flag was officially adopted in 1911.

SPECIAL FOOD

Avocado toast

Welcome to California!

The third-largest state! The word California is from a Spanish novel published back in 1510. The name of this novel, written by Garci Rodríguez de Montalvo, was called *Las Sergas de Esplandián (The Adventures of Esplandián)*. It was about a mythical island named California that was ruled by the powerful Queen Calafia, and the writer took this name most likely from *khalif* or *khalifa,* which is an Arabic word meaning "successor." Come see our capital city, Sacramento, when you get a chance. The name is Spanish for "sacrament," which is named for the Lord's Supper or Holy Communion.

AUG California 2012

6TRJ244

dmv.ca.gov

Golden Gate Bridge

CALIFORNIA U.S.A NOV 3 8PM

CALIFORNIA

Yosemite Falls

DID YOU KNOW?

- One of the most photographed places in the world is the Golden Gate Bridge in San Francisco. It first opened in 1937, and it is still one of the longest suspension bridges ever built.

- California is a major producer of food for the United States and the world. The farmers and ranchers here produce more food by value than anywhere else.

- The tallest waterfall in North America is here in Yosemite National Park. Yosemite Falls has a large upper falls, which is a 1,430-foot drop, as well as a cascade portion and a lower falls. Altogether, the water drops some 2,425 feet!

- Want to see the largest living tree in the world? Go to Sequoia National Park. There is a tree there that has a trunk that is 102 feet in circumference!

- The very first motion picture theater opened up in Los Angeles on April 2, 1902. There are now almost 6,000 movie theaters across the country.

State bird: California valley quail

State flower: Golden Poppy

COLORADO ★ ★ ★ ★ ★

STATE STATS

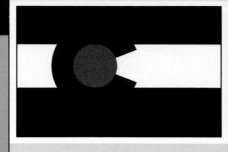

Square Miles: 104,094

Capital: Denver

Postal abbreviation: CO

U.S. region: The West

State motto: Nothing without providence

Designed by Andrew Carlisle Carson, this flag has a big letter *C* for Colorado. The colors all symbolize something, with blue for the big sky, white for the snow on the mountains, red for the clay soil, and yellow for the sunshine. It was officially adopted in 1911.

SPECIAL FOOD

Lamb chops

Nice to meet you!

There is a river that runs through our state, and the water often looks a bit red, so the name they gave the river and then our state is *colorado*, a Spanish word that means "ruddy" or "red." A good number of the largest states are here in the West, and we're ranked number 8 out of the 50 states. Our capital city is Denver, the mile-high city. It was named after a Kansas territorial governor, James Denver. Good to have you here in Colorado!

Sawatch Mountains, Leadville, Colorado

510 · IBD
'11 COLORADO

The Royal Gorge Bridge

DID YOU KNOW?

- Want to see the only city in the country that gets its water from a melting glacier? Go to Boulder, Colorado!

- The highest suspension bridge in the world goes across the Royal Gorge near Canon City. The Royal Gorge Bridge crosses the Arkansas River at the frightening height of 1,053 feet.

- We often think of Colorado being all mountains, and it does have a lot of mountains, but it also has some sand dunes that are up to 750 feet high, which are the tallest in America. Just come visit the Grand Sand Dunes National Park near Alamosa. It was created by ocean waters and wind.

Grand Sand Dunes National Park

State bird:
Lark bunting

State flower:
Rocky mountain columbine

19

CONNECTICUT ★ ★ ★

STATE STATS

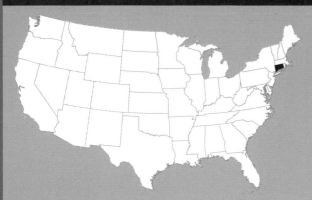

Square Miles: 5,543

Capital: Hartford

Postal abbreviation: CT

U.S. region: The Northeast

State motto: He who transplanted still sustains

The flag has a blue background with the state shield of gold and silver in the center. The white ribbon below the shield and grapevines has the state motto, *Qui Transtulit Sustinet*, which in Latin means "He Who Transplanted Still Sustains." This is referring to the first settlers of the state.

SPECIAL FOOD

Steamed cheeseburgers

How is your day?

Our state's name is originally from the native language of Algonquian, and it means "at the long tidal river." It was originally used to name a river here, the Connecticut River. At 5,543 square miles, our state is ranked 48 out of the 50. Swing by Hartford, our capital city, when you can. A ford is part of a river, and a hart is a deer, so it means "deer crossing." Glad to have you here in Connecticut!

Connecticut
AH·39871
Constitution State

Soldiers & Sailors Memorial Arch In Hartford

★ CONNECTICUT ★

West Cornwall snow covered bridge in Connecticut

DID YOU KNOW?

- People don't use them as much anymore, but the first phone book in the world was published in 1878 by the New Haven District Telephone Company. There were just 50 total names in the book!

- One of the oldest public libraries in the United States is the Scoville Memorial Library. Richard Smith, a local blast furnace owner, started the book collection in 1771. With community contributions, he was able to buy 200 books. People could borrow them and return them on the third Monday of every month.

- In 1901, the state of Connecticut passed the first automobile law. It set the speed limit at the amazing pace of 12 miles per hour. Later on, in 1937, Connecticut became the first state to issue permanent license plates for vehicles.

Pierson College Walkway, Yale University

State flower: Mountain laurel

State bird: American robin

DELAWARE ★ ★ ★ ★ ★

STATE STATS

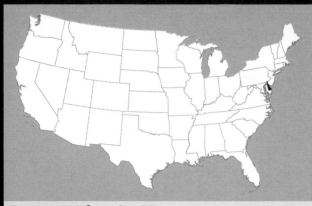

Square Miles: 2,489

Capital: Dover

Postal abbreviation: DE

U.S. region: The South

State motto: Liberty and independence

THE FIRST STATE
122222
DELAWARE 13

DECEMBER 7, 1787

The colors of the flag are colonial blue and a yellow-brown color, which were the colors of George Washington's uniform as he led the troops in the Revolutionary War. The ship on the flag represents how important the sea and ship-building are to the state. There is a soldier who stands for the right of citizens to bear arms and a farmer who stands for the importance of agriculture.

SPECIAL FOOD

Scrapple

Hi there!

Our state's name comes from a person's name. Lord de la Warr, which is French for "of the war," had the Delaware River named after him and then the state. At 2,489 square miles, we rank 49 out of 50, almost the smallest state! Dover is our capital and the second-largest city in the state. It's an ancient word that means "waters" and was named after a place called Dover in England. So glad to have you here in Delaware.

NASCAR racing at Dover International Speedway

Cape Henlopen State
Park — Great Dune

DID YOU KNOW?

- Why do they call Delaware "The First State"? Well, it was the first of the 13 colonies to approve the United States Constitution on December 7, 1787.

- How big is your frying pan at home? The one made for the Delmarva Chicken Festival in 1950 is 10 feet in diameter, and it can hold up to 180 gallons of oil, as well as 800 chicken quarters.

- You can see the 80-foot Great Dune in Cape Henlopen State Park. Just come on over to Lewes!

State flower: Peach blossom

State bird: Blue hen chicken

23

FLORIDA ★ ★ ★ ★ ★ ★ ★

STATE STATS

Square Miles: 65,758

Capital: Tallahassee

Postal abbreviation: FL

U.S. region: The South

State motto: In God we trust

Though it used to be just white with the state seal in the middle, now the flag has a white background with red stripes and the state seal in the center. The red is St. Andrew's cross. On the seal are a Seminole woman, a palm tree, and the sun.

SPECIAL FOOD

Key lime pie

Let's spend a day at the beach!

Did you know that our state's name is Spanish and means "flowery Easter" or "feast of flowers"? The Spanish people who first came to Florida realized it was Easter time, the time we celebrate Jesus' Resurrection. We are the 22nd-largest state in the U.S. at 65,758 square miles. Our capital city is Tallahassee, which is a native word that means "old town" or "old fields." Welcome to Florida!

MYFLORIDA.COM

DECAL

SAMPLE

SUNSHINE STATE

DID YOU KNOW?

- St. Augustine is known as the oldest permanent city in the U.S. It was settled long ago in 1565 by Europeans who had sailed the Atlantic Ocean.

- You can tour the amazing Kennedy Space Center at Cape Canaveral. Most of the spacecraft that have been launched into space came from here, including the first space shuttle in 1981.

- Most rivers flow south, but the St. Johns River is one of the few rivers that flows north.

- If you go to the Everglades, you will be in the largest subtropical wilderness in the United States.

- The longest river sailboat race in the world goes from Palatka to Jacksonville along the St. Johns River. The Annual Mug Race runs 38½ miles!

State bird:
Mockingbird

State flower:
Orange blossom

GEORGIA ★ ★ ★ ★ ★ ★ ★

STATE STATS

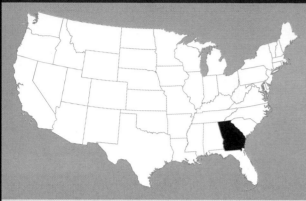

Square Miles: 59,425

Capital: Atlanta

Postal abbreviation: GA

U.S. region: The South

State motto: Wisdom, Justice, Moderation

On the upper left-hand corner of the flag is the state seal on a blue background, with 13 stars standing for the original 13 colonies, two red stripes, and one white stripe. It has changed more than any other U.S. flag.

SPECIAL FOOD

Boiled peanuts

Hello there, friend!

It's interesting to learn that our state was named in honor of King George II of Great Britain. The name "George" comes from Greek and basically means "farmer." Our capital city, Atlanta, was named for the Western and Atlantic Railroad depot that was very significant here in the South way back. We rank in size with the other states as 24 out of 50. A lot of people know Georgia for our famous peaches, which first came here in the 17th century. Enjoy your stay!

Peach State GEORGIA
PXE9860
GRADY — AUG 15

Live Oak Trees
Georgia

DID YOU KNOW?

- Are you able to eat peanuts? Though some people are very allergic, there are a lot of people who can eat peanuts and peanut butter. In fact, Georgia produces over two billion pounds of them every year.

- Granite is a type of very hard, igneous rock. If you go to Stone Mountain near Atlanta, you will see one of the single largest masses of visible granite in the whole world.

- Blackbeard Island Wilderness Area was protected by Congress in 1975. It covers about 3,000 acres. Edward "Blackbeard" Teach, a pirate from long ago, was known to spend time here and may have buried treasure in the area!

State flower: Cherokee rose

State bird: Brown thrasher

27

HAWAII ★ ★ ★ ★ ★ ★ ★ ★ ★ ★

STATE STATS

Square Miles: 10,932

Capital: Honolulu

Postal abbreviation: HI

U.S. region: The West

State motto: The life of the land is perpetuated in righteousness

The Union Jack in the upper left-hand side of the flag stands for Hawaii's connection to Great Britain. In fact, the flag was designed in Great Britain for Hawaii's King Kamehameha back in 1798. The three white stripes, two blue stripes, and three red stripes stand for the eight main islands of Hawaii.

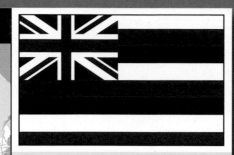

SPECIAL FOOD — Hawaiian shave ice

Aloha from Hawaii!

Here on our islands there is a language we speak called Hawaiian. In that language, we speak of a special homeland of the Polynesian people who live here now, and that place is called Hawaiki. This is part of where our state name comes from. There is a second part that says in legend that Hawai'iloa discovered these islands. Though we seem small, at 10,932 square miles, we rank 43 out of the 50 states. The name of our capital city is Honolulu, which means "a sheltered harbor." Aloha from Hawaii!

HAWAII
MNG 728
- ALOHA STATE -

Kahoolawe is the smallest of the eight main volcanic islands.

DID YOU KNOW?

- Hawaii isn't just one island or a few islands close together. It's a collection of 136 islands.

- If you go to Mount Waialeale (why-ALL-lay-all-lay), you'll be standing on one of the wettest places in the United States. It rains about 460 inches a year, which is around 38 feet of rain!

- The ukulele has come to represent the sound of the islands. It looks like a small guitar with four strings and was introduced to Hawaii from Portugal.

- Thought to be the only carnivorous caterpillars in the world, these small creatures in Hawaii called Eupithecia look like twigs and will snatch flies as they fly by!

- Hawaii is a long way from anywhere! It is said to be the most isolated population center on earth. The closest major area is California, some 2,390 miles away.

State bird: Nene (Hawaiian goose)

State flower: Yellow hibiscus

29

IDAHO ★ ★ ★ ★ ★ ★ ★ ★ ★ ★

STATE STATS

Square Miles: 83,569

Capital: Boise

Postal abbreviation: ID

U.S. region: The West

State motto: Let it be perpetual

The state seal of Idaho is centered on the flag with a blue background. It's the only state seal designed by a woman. Her name was Emma Edwards Green. Symbols on the flag include a woman who stands for justice, as well as images of agriculture, mining, mountains, forestry, and more.

SPECIAL FOOD

Ice cream potato

Greetings from Idaho!

We have a rather interesting origin for our state's name. Long ago, there was someone named George Willing who said the name was from a native language and meant something like "gem of the mountains." However, it was found later that he simply made it up! Our state is 83,569 square miles, which makes us the 14th-largest state. Come visit our capital city, Boise, when you can. The name is French and refers to the beautiful woods here.

Downtown Boise

Scenic IDAHO
1A WJ785
FAMOUS POTATOES 02

Hell's Canyon

DID YOU KNOW?

- If you want to see the deepest gorge in America, come to Hell's Canyon.

- Come to Soda Springs to see the largest man-made geyser in the world. In 1937, a local man was drilling in search of water for a pool. When the drill got 315 feet down, he broke through a chamber that still shoots water 150 feet high on windless days!

- Back in 1924, Cory Engen, an Olympic ski champ, started a celebration to help curb boredom during the long winters in the town of McCall. The Winter Carnival still happens each year.

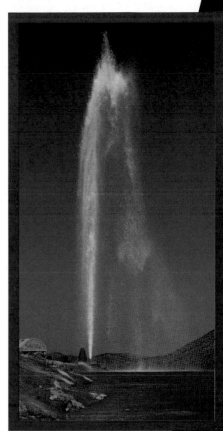

McCall Winter Carnival

State flower: Syringa

State bird: Mountain bluebird

ILLINOIS ★ ★ ★ ★ ★ ★ ★ ★

STATE STATS

Square Miles: 57,914

Capital: Springfield

Postal abbreviation: IL

U.S. region: The Midwest

State motto: State Sovereignty, National Union

ILLINOIS

The background color of the flag is white, with the seal of the state in the center. The eagle stands for the United States, and it's holding the state motto, which is "State Sovereignty, National Union." The name Illinois was added to the flag in 1970.

SPECIAL FOOD

Chicago-style hot dog

Hey y'all!

Our state's name is a mixture of native Algonquian and French. There are several possible meanings, including "men," "superior men," or even "speaks normally." We are the 25th-largest state out of 50 at 57,914 square miles. Our capital is Springfield, and if you look at a map, you'll see that it's kind of in the middle of the state. It's so nice to have you here in Illinois!

Corn and soybean fields near Royal, Illinois

ILLINOIS 10-18
AP 75117
LAND OF LINCOLN

Navy Pier, Chicago

DID YOU KNOW?

- The world's very first skyscraper was built in Chicago in 1885. It was the Home Insurance Building, and it was a whopping 10 stories high!

- Have you ever been on a Ferris wheel? Well, the person who invented it was George W. Ferris, and the first one was started up at Chicago's 1893 World Exposition.

- The same year that the Ferris wheel started up, the first aquarium in Illinois opened in Chicago.

- The story about the first ice cream sundae is a little muddled, but it's said that the first one was made in Evanston. The town leaders didn't want people hanging out at the soda fountain on Sundays, so they prohibited the sale of ice cream sodas on that day. Then they began selling ice cream without the soda and began calling it a sundae.

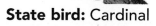

State flower: Native Violet

State bird: Cardinal

33

INDIANA ★ ★ ★ ★ ★ ★ ★ ★

STATE STATS

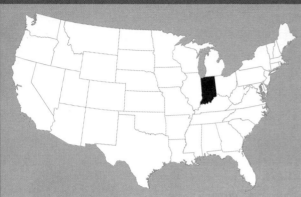

Square Miles: 36,420

Capital: Indianapolis

Postal abbreviation: IN

U.S. region: The Midwest

State motto: The crossroads of America

Paul Hadley won a flag contest, and his design became the official flag in 1917. There is a blue background with a circle of 13 stars that stand for the original 13 colonies, while the 5 stars within the circle stand for the next 5 states that became a part of the nation, and the large star above the torch stands for Indiana, the 19th state. The torch represents liberty.

SPECIAL FOOD

Sugar cream pie

Hi there!

Our state name means "land of the Indians," which traces its roots back to Latin, then all the way back to the Persian language, referring to the Indus River of India. That's a long journey for a name! Our capital is Indianapolis, which is the state name and the Greek word *polis* (city) put together. We are the 38th-largest state, and you can find us in the Midwest. Take care, friend!

00-00 **INDIANA** 00
123ABC
00

DID YOU KNOW?

- Ever heard of the Raggedy-Ann doll? These dolls were created in 1915 by Johnny Gruelle of Indianapolis.

- The first-ever professional league baseball game was played on May 4, 1871. It was a National Association game between the Cleveland Forest Cities and Ft. Wayne Kekiongas, and the Kekiongas won!

- The Indy 500 has the highest attendance of any other single-day sports event in the world: 300,000 people! It's a 500-mile auto race that started in 1911. Sometimes the track area is called the brickyard because it used to be paved with bricks.

State flower: Peony

State bird: Cardinal

IOWA ★ ★ ★ ★ ★ ★ ★ ★ ★ ★ ★ ★

STATE STATS

Square Miles: 56,273

Capital: Des Moines

Postal abbreviation: IA

U.S. region: The Midwest

State motto: Our liberties we prize and our rights we will maintain

IOWA

This flag was designed by Dixie Cornell Gebhardt and became the state flag in 1921. The red stripe represents courage, the white stripe represents purity, and the blue stripe represents loyalty and justice, while all the stripes reflect the French history of the state. The eagle holds a ribbon with the state motto, "Our liberties we prize and our rights we will maintain."

SPECIAL FOOD

Sweet corn

Mississippi River, Bellevue, Iowa

Hello, friend!

Our state is named after the Native Iowa people who lived here. The name could mean "sleepy ones" or "beautiful land." Iowa is ranked 26th largest out of the 50 states at 56,273 square miles. The capital city is Des Moines, which was originally Fort Des Moines. Des Moines is French for "the monks." So good to have you here in Iowa!

IOWA

CPG 699

• POTTAWATTAMIE •

DID YOU KNOW?

- If you want to see the world's steepest and shortest railway, come on over to Fenlon Place Elevator in Dubuque.

- With the Missouri River on the west and the Mississippi River on the east, Iowa is the only state whose east and west borders are formed by water alone.

- During the Ice Age after the great Flood, this area was covered in snow and ice. It was also abundant with woolly mammoths. Their bones are found everywhere here. Some of the first bones were found by a local family picking for berries on their land.

State flower: Wild rose

State bird: Eastern goldfinch

KANSAS ★ ★ ★ ★ ★ ★ ★ ★ ★ ★

STATE STATS

Square Miles: 82,278

Capital: Topeka

Postal abbreviation: KS

U.S. region: The Midwest

State motto: To the stars through difficulties

KANSAS

The 34 stars on the flag represent the states at the time Kansas became the 34th state. You can also find the state motto (*Ad astra per aspera*, or "To the stars through difficulties"), a sunflower, a farmer, a steamboat, natives hunting buffalo, and a wagon train. These are all symbols of the history of Kansas.

SPECIAL FOOD

Barbecue ribs

RL ·KANSAS· KS 2017
540 KFG

It's nice to meet you!

Kansas was the name of the river here before the state, but it was the name of the Kaw or Kansas tribe before that. It is a word that is connected to the winds. Topeka, our capital city, is also a native word. It means something like "a good place to dig potatoes." Guess you know what they grew here! Out of all the states, we rank the 15th largest.

Sunflower field in full bloom

KANSAS U.S.A.

KANSAS ★ ★

**Keeper of the Plains
Wichita, Kansas**

DID YOU KNOW?

- The *Shawnee Sun*, first published in 1835, was the first newspaper that was printed entirely in a Native American language (Algonquian).

- The very first female mayor in the United States was Susanna Madora Salter. She was elected in Argonia, Kansas, in 1887.

- Amelia Earhart was from Atchison, Kansas. She was the first female aviator to have a solo flight across the Atlantic Ocean and the first person to fly solo across the Pacific Ocean between Hawaii and California, some 2,408 miles.

State flower: Sunflower

State bird: Western meadowlark

39

KENTUCKY ★ ★ ★ ★ ★ ★ ★

STATE STATS

Square Miles: 40,408

Capital: Frankfort

Postal abbreviation: KY

U.S. region: The South

State motto: United we stand, divided we fall

Blue, yellow, and white are the main colors of the flag. The state motto says, "United We Stand, Divided We Fall," and the picture within the circle is of two men shaking hands in an agreement. The state's flower, the goldenrod, is also on the flag.

SPECIAL FOOD

Kentucky Hot brown

Welcome to Kentucky!

Like some other states, the name Kentucky first referred to a river. It was from the original Iroquoian language, meaning possibly "the land," "the prairie," or "the meadow." The capital city's name has an interesting history. Stephen Frank, a pioneer here in the 1780s, was killed near a ford of the Kentucky River. After that, they called the area Frank's Ford, which later became Frankfort. At 40,408 square miles, we're the 37th-largest state.

Frankfort, Kentucky

Kentucky
UNBRIDLED SPIRIT
333 XDB
CAMPBELL 02:18

DID YOU KNOW?

- The first horse race at Churchill Downs in Louisville was in 1875. The Kentucky Derby has become the most famous horse race in the world.

- Derby pie is a famously delicious chocolate and walnut pastry that they make for the Kentucky Derby.

- Kaelin's restaurant in Louisville claims that the first cheeseburger was served here. The date? Well, that would be in 1934!

- Mammoth Cave near Brownsville is the world's longest cave. It's around 400 miles in length!

- There is a United States Army post in Kentucky called Fort Knox, which is adjacent to the United States Bullion Depository. That's a fancy way of saying it has a large portion of the United States' gold reserves there, just south of Louisville.

State flower: Goldenrod

State bird: Cardinal

41

LOUISIANA ★ ★ ★ ★ ★ ★ ★ ★ ★ ★

STATE STATS

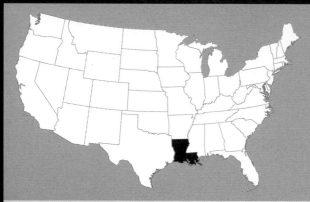

Square Miles: 52,378

Capital: Baton Rouge

Postal abbreviation: LA

U.S. region: The South

State motto: Union, Justice and Confidence

The state's coat of arms is at the center of this flag, with the blue background showing a pelican giving food to its young ones, and the state motto underneath them: "Union, Justice and Confidence."

🍴 SPECIAL FOOD

Jambalaya

Hi!
Our state was named after a person — King Louis XIV of France, to be exact. His name meant "heard of" or "famous." And the name Baton Rouge, our capital? It means "red stick" in French. We are ranked as the 31st-largest state at 52,378 square miles. If you're traveling through the South, come see Louisiana with me!

★ LOUISIANA ★

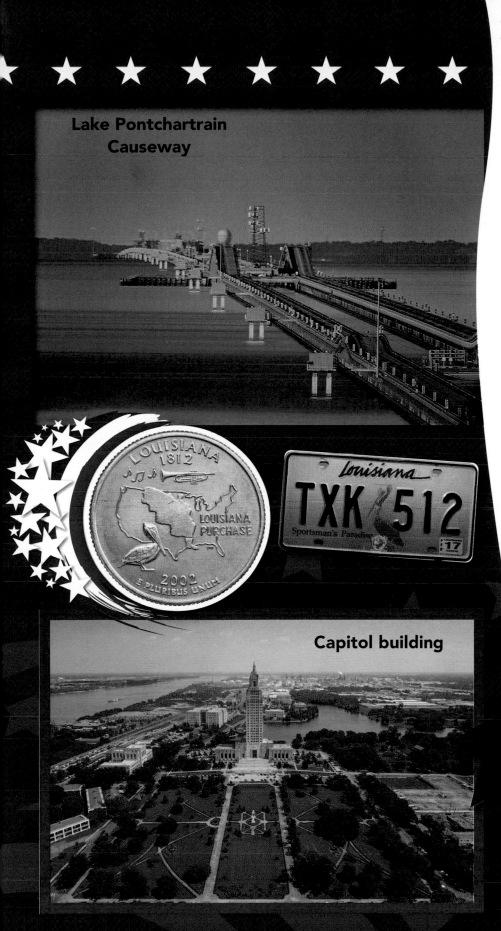

Lake Pontchartrain Causeway

Capitol building

DID YOU KNOW?

- There are only two states that do not have counties. One of them is Louisiana, which has political subdivisions called parishes. The other is Alaska, which is divided into boroughs.

- The longest bridge over continuous water in the world is the Lake Pontchartrain Causeway. It connects Metairie with St. Tammany Parish on the North Shore, and it's 24 miles long. It's so long in fact that you can see it bending over the curvature of the Earth's horizon!

Crawfish

- Louisiana has the tallest state capitol building in the U.S. It's in Baton Rouge, is 450 feet high, and has 34 floors.

State flower: Magnolia

State bird: Eastern brown pelican

43

STATE STATS

Square Miles: 35,380

Capital: Augusta

Postal abbreviation: ME

U.S. region: The Northeast

State motto: I lead

On this mainly blue flag is a star at the top that stands for the North Star with the word *Dirigo* beneath it, which means "I lead." The farmer and the sailor represent the early settlers of the state and their main industries. The moose is the state animal, and the white pine is the state tree.

SPECIAL FOOD

Lobster

Hello there!

It might seem too obvious, but it's possible our state's name simply refers to the mainland rather than the islands off the coast. There is also a province in France named Mayne that it could refer to as well. No one is quite sure. In 1797, the area that became our capital city was renamed Augusta after Augusta Dearborn. She was the daughter of a significant military man in the Revolutionary War, Henry Dearborn. We may be small, ranked 39th largest state out of the 50, but we have a great history. Greetings from the great state of Maine!

MAINE • APR
6992 LH

**Bull Moose
Baxter State Park**

MAINE U.S.A. NOV 3 8PM

MAINE

Sunrise in
Acadia National Park

DID YOU KNOW?

- There is a very famous path called the Appalachian Trail that runs from Maine to Georgia. The trail is 2,190 miles long. It is such a beautiful display of God's creation!

- Maine is farther northeast than any other state, and Eastport is the most eastern city in the United States. This city is made up completely of islands.

- If you go up the Cadillac Mountain in Acadia National Park, you'll be the first to see the sunlight of each new day in America.

Lobster boats in Portland, Maine

- Do you like seafood? How about lobster? Well, almost 60,000 tons of lobster are caught off the coast of Maine every year.

State flower: White pinecone and tassel

State bird: Chickadee

45

MARYLAND ★ ★ ★ ★ ★

STATE STATS

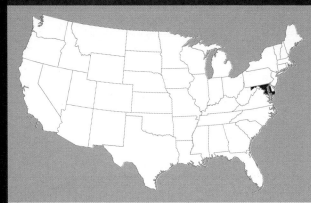

Square Miles: 12,406

Capital: Annapolis

Postal abbreviation: MD

U.S. region: The South

State motto: Manly deeds, womanly words

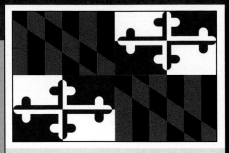

Lord Baltimore helped found the colony of Maryland, and so the symbols on the flag are family shields — the black and gold for his father's side, the Calverts, and the white and red for his mother's side, the Crosslands.

SPECIAL FOOD

Berger cookies

Hi!

Our state's name has a long history. We were named after Queen Henrietta Maria, who was the wife of King Charles I of England. But the name Mary goes so much further back. In Hebrew, the language of the Old Testament, it meant "bitterness." The name Annapolis, our capital city, was named after a royal person, Princess Anne of Denmark and Norway. Who knew that we would become the 42nd-largest state in the U.S.? Thanks for coming to Maryland!

Maryland
MD PROUD

Downtown Annapolis —Maryland State House

DID YOU KNOW?

- The oldest surviving railroad station in the country is found in Baltimore. It's called the B & O Railroad Museum.

- "The Star-Spangled Banner," the national anthem of the United States, was written by Francis Scott Key. He wrote it in 1814 after American forces fought off a British attack at Fort McHenry, Maryland.

- You can see wild ponies living on Assateague Island. People believe the ancestors of these horses swam ashore after a Spanish galleon was shipwrecked here in the 1600s.

- Built in 1772, the oldest state capital still in continuous legislative use is the Maryland State House in Annapolis. It's also the only state house that was ever used as the nation's capital.

Chesapeake Bay's Tangier Island

- If you like seafood, you'll find a lot of it here. Maryland's a big producer and processor of seafood and a national leader in the production of clams and blue crabs. Half of all the blue crab harvest comes from the Chesapeake Bay area.

Wild Ponies, Assateague Island

State flower: Black-eyed Susan

State bird: Baltimore oriole

MASSACHUSETTS ★

STATE STATS

Square Miles: 10,554

Capital: Boston

Postal abbreviation: MA

U.S. region: The Northeast

State motto: By the sword we seek peace, but peace only under liberty

On this white flag is the state seal with a star, which stands for the fact that Massachusetts was part of the original 13 states. The name of the state comes from a Native American word, so the image of the Native American represents this connection. The sword and the arm remind us of the state's motto, "By the sword we seek peace, but peace only under liberty," which is written on the flag in Latin.

SPECIAL FOOD — **Clam chowder**

Greetings

The name Massachusetts is an Algonquian name meaning "people of the great hills" or "at the great hill." Our capital city, Boston, has been around a long time. It was founded by Puritan settlers from England in 1630. Of all the states, we rank 44th out of 50 in size. Come have a look around our northeastern state!

★ MASSACHUSETTS ★

Sankaty Lighthouse

FEB ⋆ Massachusetts ⋆ 11
215 BG2
The Spirit of America

Old South Church

DID YOU KNOW?

- The very first Thanksgiving Day was celebrated in Plymouth in 1621. This was a celebration of the harvest that lasted three whole days. There were 53 pilgrims there along with 90 Wampanoag people.

- The town of Princeton was named after the Reverend Thomas Prince. He was the pastor of the Old South Church in Boston. The school, Princeton University, was chartered in 1746 and was created to train ministers.

- The telephone was invented in Boston by Alexander Graham Bell in 1876. Wouldn't he be surprised at today's phones!

- You can tour a replica of the *Mayflower*. That was the ship the Pilgrims sailed over on. They loved popcorn so much that they ate it for breakfast!

Mayflower II

MASSACHUSETTS 1788
THE BAY STATE
2000
E PLURIBUS UNUM

Beach at Provincetown, Cape Cod

State flower: Mayflower

State bird: Chickadee

49

MICHIGAN ★ ★ ★ ★ ★ ★

STATE STATS

Square Miles: 96,714

Capital: Lansing

Postal abbreviation: MI

U.S. region: The Midwest

State motto: If you seek a pleasant peninsula, look about you

In the center of the flag is the coat of arms with a man raising his hand, which stands for peace, while the gun in his other hand stands for the right to bear arms. The moose and elk shown are a part of the state's symbols, and the eagle holding the olive branch and arrows represents the United States.

SPECIAL FOOD

Detroit pizza

Happy to see you.

Did you know the name of our state means "large water" or "large lake"? It's from the native language of Ojibwe (oh-JIB-way). And do you know why our capital is named Lansing? Well, in 1836, some people from Lansing, New York, were tricked into coming to the area where Lansing, Michigan, was supposed to be. Even though they found nothing here, they stayed and named the area after the city they moved from. We're a pretty big state, especially for the Midwest, and rank 11th out of all the states.

Harvesting cranberries in the Upper Penisula

PURE Michigan
SEP
DJV 1825
michigan.org

50

Ice Cave & Ice Curtains on Grand Island near Munising, Michigan

MICHIGAN 1837 GREAT LAKES STATE 2004 E PLURIBUS UNUM

Mackinac Bridge

DID YOU KNOW?

- One of the oldest European settlements in the United States is Sault Ste. Marie. It was founded in 1668 by Father Jacques Marquette.

- The Indian River is home to one of the largest crucifixes in the world. It's 55 feet tall and called the Cross in the Woods.

- One of the longest suspension bridges in the world is the Mackinac Bridge. It spans a whopping 5 miles over the Straits of Mackinac, which is where Lake Huron and Lake Michigan meet. Called the Mighty Mac, it took three years to construct and was first opened in 1957.

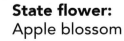

State flower:
Apple blossom

State bird:
Robin

51

MINNESOTA ★ ★ ★ ★ ★

STATE STATS

Square Miles: 86,936

Capital: St. Paul

Postal abbreviation: MN

U.S. region: The Midwest

State motto: The star of the north

On the flag, there are 19 stars that represent Minnesota's statehood, 19 states after the original 13. The larger star stands for the North Star, and that's why the French words "*l'etoile du nord*," "star of the north," are written on the flag. It also stands for Minnesota.

SPECIAL FOOD

Hotdish

How are you?

The name of our state was first the name of the river, and it means "cloudy water" or "sky-tinted water" in the native language of the Dakota people. Once named Pig's Eye, the name of our capital was changed to St. Paul, honoring the saint in the Bible and a much better name! Our state ranks 12th largest of the states at 86,936 square miles. I hope you enjoy your time here.

EXPLORE Minnesota.com
457 ★ MKZ
SEP • 10,000 lakes • 14

People ice skating on a frozen waterway

DID YOU KNOW?

- In 1898, the Kensington Runestone was found near Alexandria on the farm of Olaf Ohman. Weighing in at 202 pounds, the stone allegedly told the journey of a group of Vikings in 1362. Some still believe the stone is just a hoax.

- The largest professional dinner theater in the U.S. is said to be Chanhassen Dinner Theatres in Minneapolis-Saint Paul.

- The great Mississippi River starts in Lake Itasca and travels all the way to the Gulf of Mexico.

- The largest mall in the nation is called the Mall of America. Opened in 1992, it has hundreds of stores, an aquarium, and an indoor theme park!

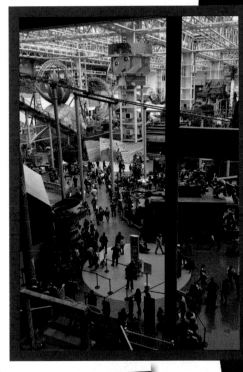

State flower: Pink and white lady's slipper

State bird: Common loon

MISSISSIPPI ★ ★ ★ ★ ★

STATE STATS

Square Miles: 48,432

Capital: Jackson

Postal abbreviation: MS

U.S. region: The South

State motto: By valor and arms

As of 2020, a new flag features a magnolia blossom (the state flower), surrounded by 20 white stars representing Mississippi as the 20th state, a gold star standing for the state's native tribes, and the words "In God We Trust."

IN GOD WE TRUST

SPECIAL FOOD

Mud pie

Hello!

The name Mississippi is a word in the native Ojibwe language, and it means "great river" or "father of waters" in reference to the Mississippi River. Our capital city, Jackson, was named after General Andrew Jackson. He later became a U.S. president. Of all the states, we rank 32nd in size. So glad you could come to Mississippi!

MISSISSIPPI

AAA 0000

LAUDERDALE

Pass Christian, Mississippi Gulf

MISSISSIPPI USA NOV 3 8 PM

★ MISSISSIPPI ★

**Natchez Trace Parkway
Pharr Mounds, Mississippi**

Mississippi Cottonfield

DID YOU KNOW?

- If you are walking anywhere along the 440-mile Natchez Trace, you'll be walking on a trail once used by the native people of the area.

- In 1870, Hiram R. Revels became the very first African American senator.

- The largest Bible repair plant in the nation is the Norris Bookbinding Company, located in Greenwood.

- In 1902, while he was on a hunting expedition near Onward, Mississippi, President Theodore (Teddy) Roosevelt refused to shoot a captured bear. Some men had tied it up to a tree so it would be easy for him to shoot. When people heard of this, it resulted in the creation of the world-famous "Teddy" bear in honor of the president.

- Since the town of Vicksburg was located right along the Mississippi River, Abraham Lincoln said it was the key to winning the Civil War because the river was a major means of transportation.

State flower: Magnolia

State bird: Northern mockingbird

MISSOURI ★ ★ ★ ★ ★ ★ ★

STATE STATS

Square Miles: 69,707

Capital: Jefferson City

Postal abbreviation: MO

U.S. region: The Midwest

State motto: The welfare of the people shall be the supreme law

Designed by Marie Elizabeth Oliver in 1908, there are three horizontal stripes on the Missouri flag. These stripes stand for purity (white), justice (blue), and valor and bravery (red). There is a new moon that stands for the new state being formed, while the eagle stands for the national federal government, and the bear stands for courage. If you count the stars, you'll find 24, as Missouri was the 24th state.

SPECIAL FOOD

Toasted ravioli

MO2 021
AUG MISSOURI BICENTENNIAL
1821 ★ 2021

Railroad Katy Bridge at Boonville over Missouri River

Hi, nice to meet you here!

The name of our state came from the native peoples who were here long ago. The word is from the Illinois language, and Missouri means "town of large canoes" or "dugout canoe." Our capital, Jefferson City (or Jeff City), is named after the third president, Thomas Jefferson. Out of all the states, we rank 21st largest at 69,707 square miles. Enjoy your stay!

**Route 66
Steak 'n Shake**

**Alley Springs Mill
in Ozark National
Scenic Riverways**

- Richard Blechynde served tea with ice at the St. Louis World's fair in 1904. This helped make iced tea popular, though the recipe was printed in a cookbook as early as 1879.

- Do you like ice cream cones? Well, they were sold before but became more popular when sold at the 1904 World's Fair in St. Louis.

- The first successful parachute jump out of a moving airplane is said by many to be by Captain Albert Berry at Jefferson Barracks, Missouri, in 1912.

**Gateway Arch,
June 1965**

- The Gateway Arch is in St. Louis. It was finished in 1965, is 630 feet tall, and was built to sway in the wind as much as 18 inches! It's the tallest man-made monument in the country.

State flower:
White hawthorn

State bird:
Eastern bluebird

57

MONTANA ★ ★ ★ ★ ★ ★ ★ ★

STATE STATS

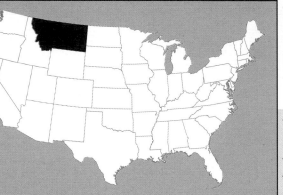

Square Miles: 147,040

Capital: Helena

Postal abbreviation: MT

U.S. region: The West

State motto: Gold and silver

The state seal of Montana is at the center of the flag with the name of the state at the top. Both farmers, represented by the plow, and miners, represented by the pick and shovel, helped settle Montana and are shown with the state's landscape. Montana's motto is also shown, which is *Oro y plata*, "Gold and silver."

SPECIAL FOOD

Bison burgers

MONTANA
7·56976B

Welcome!

Our name comes from the Spanish people who first settled in this area of the country. In Spanish, *montaña* means "mountain." If you visit Helena, our capital city, it's fun to know why it was named that. A group of people were sitting around in 1864 coming up with names for the place, and someone thought it should be called Helena (He-LEE-nah) after Helena Township in Minnesota. Well, a few others thought it should be Helena (HEL-ih-nah) after Helena, Arkansas. The pronunciation wasn't fixed until 1882 as HEL-ih-nah! Come enjoy Montana, the 4th-largest state in the country.

Capital Dome, Helena Montana State Building

MONTANA U.S.
NOV 3
8PM

★ MONTANA ★

Triple Divide Peak in Glacier National Park

A family ranch in Big Timber, Montana

DID YOU KNOW?

- Montana has what some call a triple divide. This is a single place in North America that allows water to flow into three major areas, which, in this case, is the Pacific Ocean, the Atlantic Ocean, and Hudson Bay. You can see this phenomenon at Triple Divide Peak in Glacier National Park.

- Yellowstone National Park in southern Montana and northern Wyoming was the very first national park in the nation. Established in 1872, it also happens to be the first national park in the world.

- Grasshopper Glacier was discovered back in the early 1900s by a geologist named J.P. Kimball. It gets its bizarre appearance from tens of millions of grasshoppers — locusts, actually — frozen in the ice. Kimball sent samples of the insect to the U.S. Bureau of Entomology in 1914, and they realized that they were Rocky Mountain locusts, a type of locust that had been extinct for over a century.

State flower: Bitterroot

State bird: Western meadowlark

NEBRASKA ★ ★ ★ ★ ★ ★ ★

STATE STATS

Square Miles: 77,348

Capital: Lincoln

Postal abbreviation: NE

U.S. region: The Midwest

State motto: Equality before the law

In the state seal that is on the flag, there are a lot of symbols that help us understand Nebraska's history. There is wheat that stands for farming, a blacksmith that stands for industrialization, a cabin that stands for the first settlers, and a railroad and steamboat that stand for transportation.

SPECIAL FOOD — **Runza**

How is your day?

Hope it's good! Our state's name is a native Oto word and means "flat water" or "flattened water" after the Platte River. The city that became our capital was once called Lancaster, but the name was changed to honor President Lincoln. Out of all the states, we rank as 16th largest. Glad you could come to the Midwest and visit Nebraska!

NEBRASKA 1
9-C9287
1867 2017

Nebraska cornfield and grain elevator

NEBRASKA

Spider Monkey in the Lied Jungle

Chimney Rock

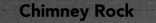

DID YOU KNOW?

- Chimney Rock rises up some 300 feet above the surrounding plains. It was used as a marker for those traveling the Oregon Trail during the 19th century.

- The Lied Jungle that is located in the Henry Doorly Zoo in Omaha is the nation's largest indoor rainforest. They opened it in 1992.

- In 1917, Father Edward Flanagan opened a home in Omaha to help troubled boys. He had been helping homeless men but wanted to see if he could reach them before they were lost on the streets.

Original site of "Boy's Town."

State flower: Tall Goldenrod

State bird: Western meadowlark

NEVADA ★ ★ ★ ★ ★ ★ ★ ★ ★ ★ ★

STATE STATS

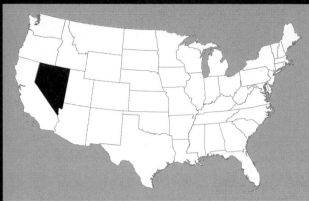

Square Miles: 110,572

Capital: Carson City

Postal abbreviation: NV

U.S. region: The West

State motto: All for our country

In 1926, Nevada had a contest to design a state flag, and Louis Schellbach III won the contest. His design included the phrase "Battle Born," reflecting the time when Nevada became a state, which was during the Civil War. Also on the flag are the state's flower, the sagebrush, and a silver star that helps people remember the silver that was mined here.

SPECIAL FOOD

Shrimp cocktail

Hi!

Nevada is a Spanish word that means "snow-capped" or "snow-covered" and refers to the snowy Sierra Nevada mountains. At 110,572 square miles, we're the 7th-largest state! Our capital, Carson City, was named after Kit Carson, who was a mountain man and scout who guided people through this area. So nice of you to come by.

NEVADA
890·H14

DID YOU KNOW?

- The longest Morse code telegram ever sent was the state constitution of Nevada. Sent across wires from Carson City to Washington, D.C., in 1864, it took approximately seven hours to send the message.

- The Hoover Dam is 726 feet tall and is the highest concrete arch dam in the United States. Once called Boulder Dam, it was built during the Great Depression, starting construction in 1931 and finishing in 1936. It was one of the largest public works projects in the history of the country and employed some 5,000 workers.

- Hoover Dam helps contain Lake Mead, the largest reservoir in America.

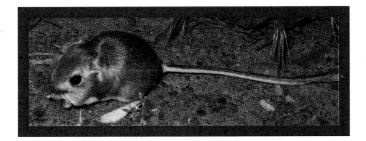

- In Death Valley, the kangaroo rat can go its entire life without drinking a drop of water. It gets liquid from all the seeds that it eats.

State flower: Sagebrush

State bird: Mountain bluebird

63

NEW HAMPSHIRE ★

STATE STATS

Square Miles: 9,349

Capital: Concord

Postal abbreviation: NH

U.S. region: The Northeast

State motto: Live free or die

The symbols on the dark blue flag include nine stars that help people remember New Hampshire was the 9th state, a rising sun showing hope, and a boulder, which stands for the granite that was a big part of the economy. The ship on the flag is the *Raleigh*, which was built during the Revolutionary War to help fight against the British.

SPECIAL FOOD

Poutine

LIVE FREE OR DIE

305 4929

6 — New HAMPSHIRE 2012

How're things?

Hopefully good! Well, the county of Hampshire in England was the inspiration for our state's name. It's an English word that means "village." We're one of the smallest states. At just 9,349 square miles, we're ranked 46 out of 50. Long ago in 1765, there were people fighting over this area, so the governor of the area named the city that would become our capital Concord. The name means agreement or harmony between people. May you find peace here today!

Portsmouth, New Hampshire

Mount Washington

LIVE FREE OR DIE

NEW HAMPSHIRE 1788
OLD MAN OF THE MOUNTAIN
2000 · E PLURIBUS UNUM

NEW HAMPSHIRE · NOV 3 · 3 P · U.S.A.

★ NEW HAMPSHIRE ★

**Red covered bridge in the
White Mountains of New Hampshire**

DID YOU KNOW?

- The strongest winds ever recorded in the U.S. were on Mount Washington. In 1934, they measured winds up to 231 miles per hour here.

- They actually know when and where the first potato was planted in the United States. It was here at Londonderry Common Field in 1719! It's interesting that potatoes originally came from Peru, the Spanish brought them over to Europe, and Europeans brought them back to America. President Thomas Jefferson asked for potatoes served in the French manner in 1802 . . . some of the first French fries!

- Do you like maple syrup on your waffles or pancakes? Well, just know that it takes about 40 gallons of sap to make approximately 1 gallon of maple syrup. Sugar maple trees have the most of this sweet sugar stuff.

State flower: Purple lilac

State bird: Purple finch

NEW JERSEY ★ ★ ★ ★ ★

STATE STATS

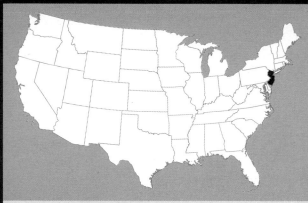

Square Miles: 8,723

Capital: Trenton

Postal abbreviation: NJ

U.S. region: The Northeast

State motto: Liberty and Prosperity

The yellow, or buff, color of this flag is similar to part of a special uniform worn by General George Washington in 1779. There on the center is the state coat of arms with New Jersey's state motto, "Liberty and Prosperity," which you see in both words and images. The woman on the left side stands for liberty, while the woman on the right stands for abundance as she holds the cornucopia. The helmet and horse on the flag stand for self-governance.

SPECIAL FOOD

Saltwater taffy

★ NEW JERSEY ★

Hello there!

Our state name comes from the French name Jersey, which happens to be the largest of the British Channel Islands. We're the 47th-largest state, so we are one of the smaller ones at 8,723 square miles. Our capital city is named Trenton, which was named after one of the leaders of the area, William Trent. It was Trent-Towne first, but they later shortened it. Welcome to New Jersey!

Atlantic City Boardwalk

DID YOU KNOW?

- The beautiful Cape May holds the distinction of being the oldest seaside resort in America. There were people from Philadelphia vacationing here in the middle of the 18th century.

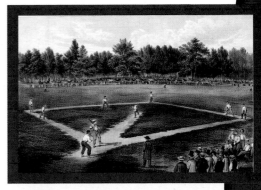

- The first mention of baseball in the U.S. was in 1791. However, the first baseball game with the modern Knickerbocker Rules was played at the Elysian Fields in Hoboken on June 19, 1846.

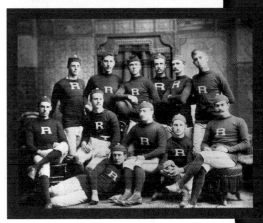

- The first intercollegiate football game was played in New Brunswick in 1869. It was Rutgers College against Princeton, and Rutgers won 6 to 4.

Lincoln Tunnel under the Hudson River, connecting Weehawken, New Jersey, with Manhattan

State flower: Blue violet

State bird: Eastern goldfinch

NEW MEXICO ★ ★ ★ ★

STATE STATS

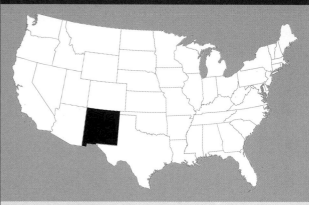

Square Miles: 121,590

Capital: Santa Fe

Postal abbreviation: NM

U.S. region: The West

State motto: It grows as it goes

The red symbol on the yellow flag comes from the Native American culture. It is called a Zia, which stands for the sun. The rays coming from the sun stand for several things, including the four directions (north, south, east, and west) and the seasons (winter, spring, summer, and fall). The red and yellow colors are similar to the flag of Spain.

SPECIAL FOOD

Frito pie

Enjoy your visit!

Welcome to New Mexico, the 5th largest of all the states! Our state's name is connected to the Aztec people, who lived here hundreds of years ago. The native people were the Mexihca, and their name became "Mexico" in Spanish. We are not certain what the name means. Santa Fe, our capital, means "holy faith" in Spanish. Our state constitution officially states that we are a bilingual state, which means we honor two languages. Though a majority of people speak English, one out of every three families here speaks Spanish at home.

999 ⊛ NNN
New Mexico USA
Land of Enchantment
0 APR 9

Sunrise over Bandelier National Monument, NM

★ NEW MEXICO ★

DID YOU KNOW?

- Some of those who live in New Mexico are descended from the Spanish people who came through here between 1598 and 1848. In fact, some who live up in the northernmost part of the state still speak a 16th-century Spanish not spoken anywhere else in the world!

- If you come here in October, go visit the city of Albuquerque. They have the world's largest international balloon fiesta. You will see nearly 600 hot air balloons and almost 1 million spectators!

- The yucca is New Mexico's state flower. The leaves can be used for so many things, like making rope, baskets, and sandals. The flower and fruit of the yucca can be eaten boiled or roasted. Mmm!

- The scientist Robert Goddard has been called the father of modern rocketry. He was originally from Massachusetts but came to Roswell, New Mexico, in 1930 to test rocket ship designs. His studies helped create the aerospace industry and are a strong part of what we do here today. Also, the crater Goddard on the Moon is named in his honor.

Adobe buildings where indigenous people are still living

State flower: Yucca

State bird: Greater roadrunner

69

NEW YORK ★ ★ ★ ★ ★ ★ ★ ★

STATE STATS

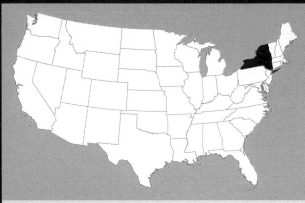

Square Miles: 54,555

Capital: Albany

Postal abbreviation: NY

U.S. region: The Northeast

State motto: Ever upward

The state flag of New York is very similar to the American Revolutionary War flag. Liberty is shown with a crown at her feet, which stands for freedom from the crown of England. Justice is shown blindfolded and carrying scales and a sword, which represents how justice should treat all fairly. The banner on the flag says *Excelsior*, which means "ever upward."

SPECIAL FOOD

New York Style Pizza

NEW YORK U.S.A
NOV 3
3 PM

★ NEW YORK ★

NEW YORK
ABC-2345
EMPIRE STATE

Greetings!

You might not know this, but the state was named after a person, the Duke of York, who eventually became King James II of England. The name itself means something like "place of yew trees." The city that would become the capital was named Albany in 1664 to honor the Duke of Albany. At 54,555 square miles, our state is ranked 27 out of 50 in size. So happy to have you here in New York!

Watkins Glen State Park

Statue of Liberty

86th Street Second Ave.
Subway Station

DID YOU KNOW?

- The copper Statue of Liberty was a gift from France in 1884. The statue was designed by the sculptor Frédéric Auguste Bartholdi, and the metal frame that supports it was built by Gustave Eiffel, the Eiffel Tower guy!

- With over 8 million people, New York City is the biggest U.S. city by population. Imagine having to travel around to work, shop, or eat out. Helping solve the problem is the subway, the nation's longest subway system!

- The *New York Post* was a paper established in 1801 by Alexander Hamilton. It's the oldest continuously running daily newspaper in the country.

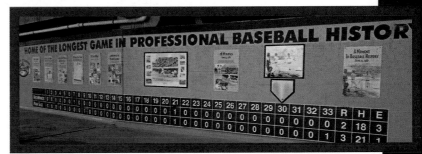

- The Rochester Red Wings played against the Pawtucket Red Sox in the longest game in professional baseball history. The game was played in 1981, went a total of 33 innings, and lasted over 8 hours! You can learn a lot more about the game at the Baseball Hall of Fame in Cooperstown.

State flower: Rose

State bird: Eastern bluebird

STATE STATS

Square Miles: 53,819

Capital: Raleigh

Postal abbreviation: NC

U.S. region: The South

State motto: To be rather than to seem

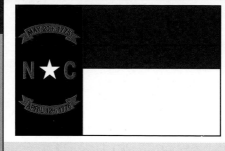

The colors of the state flag reflect the colors of the national flag. The date shown on top, May 20, 1775, stands for when one of the counties in North Carolina created an early version of the Declaration of Independence to leave Great Britain. The date on the bottom, April 12, 1776, reflects on the first official call of the colonies for freedom.

SPECIAL FOOD

Cheerwine soda

Hello!

Our state is named after King Charles I of England. Charles comes from the Frankish word *karl*, which means "man" or "husband." We're the 28th-largest state. Our capital city is known as the "City of Oaks" because of all the oak trees and was named after Sir Walter Raleigh, who helped found the Roanoke Colony in the late 1500s. Enjoy your time here in North Carolina!

Historic Yates Water Mill — Raleigh

APR NC

First in Flight

DXT-4752

NORTH CAROLINA

Hatteras Class ferry Roanoke from Cape Hatteras to Ocracoke Island, North Carolina

Venus flytrap

DID YOU KNOW?

- The University of North Carolina Chapel Hill is considered the oldest state university in the country. It first opened for students in 1795, and the first class graduated in 1798.

- In 1903, the Wright Brothers made the first successful powered flight by a person at Kill Devil Hills near Kitty Hawk. The plane flew for an amazing 12 seconds and went 120 feet. You can learn all about the achievement at the Wright Brothers National Memorial at Kitty Hawk.

- The very first English colony in America was located on Roanoke Island in 1584. Everyone mysteriously vanished with no trace except for a single word scratched on a post. The word was "Croatoan," and this was the name of the native people of the area.

- The first English child born in America was Virginia Dare. She was born in Roanoke in 1587.

- The carnivorous, or meat-eating, Venus flytrap is native to North Carolina. It captures insects and spiders that happen to touch one of the trigger hairs.

State flower: Flowering dogwood

State bird: Cardinal

73

NORTH DAKOTA ★ ★

STATE STATS

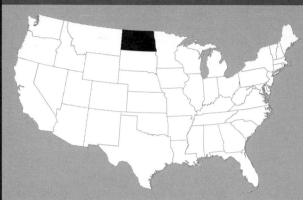

Square Miles: 70,698

Capital: Bismarck

Postal abbreviation: ND

U.S. region: The Midwest

State motto: Liberty and union, now and forever, one and inseparable

On the dark blue North Dakota flag, you can see a bald eagle holding an olive branch and arrows. On the ribbon below the eagle is written *E Pluribus Unum*, which means "Out of many, one." The stars above the eagle stand for the 13 original colonies.

SPECIAL FOOD — **Knoephla**

Welcome!

North Dakota is the 19th-largest state! The name of our state comes from a native Sioux word that means "ally" or "friend." Not a bad name! And our capital city, Bismarck, was named after the German chancellor Otto von Bismarck in 1873. Have a look around and enjoy your stay!

Buffalo in Theodore Roosevelt National Park in North Dakota

Discover the Spirit
HDW 852
NORTH DAKOTA

DID YOU KNOW?

- Do you like sunflowers? Well, North Dakota grows more sunflowers than any state other than South Dakota.

- North Dakota is home to the tallest man-made structure in the Western Hemisphere. It is the 2,063-foot KVLY-TV mast that was built in 1963 and used to be the tallest structure in the whole world.

- The explorers Lewis and Clark met Sacagawea in the upper Missouri River area of present-day North Dakota. She was the teenage girl who guided them all the way to the Pacific Ocean. They wintered here from 1804 to 1805. Sacagawea and her husband lived among the native people known as the Hidatsa and Mandan Indians.

KVLY-TV

State flower: Wild rose

State bird: Western meadowlark

OHIO ★ ★ ★ ★ ★ ★ ★ ★ ★ ★ ★ ★

STATE STATS

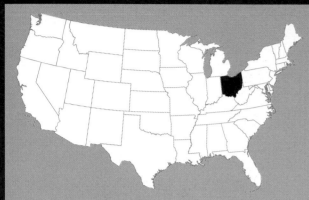

Square Miles: 44,826

Capital: Columbus

Postal abbreviation: OH

U.S. region: The Midwest

State motto: With God, all things are possible

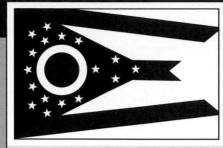

There are 17 stars on the flag, showing that Ohio was the 17th state. The "O" in the middle stands for Ohio, and the three red and two white stripes stand for roads and rivers.

SPECIAL FOOD

Five-way skyline chili

How are you?

Our state ranks as the 34th-largest state, and our state name was originally the name of our river. In fact, it's a native Seneca word that means "large creek" or "great river." The state capital, Columbus, was named after the explorer Christopher Columbus. Hope you're doing well here in the Midwest!

Columbus, Ohio

76

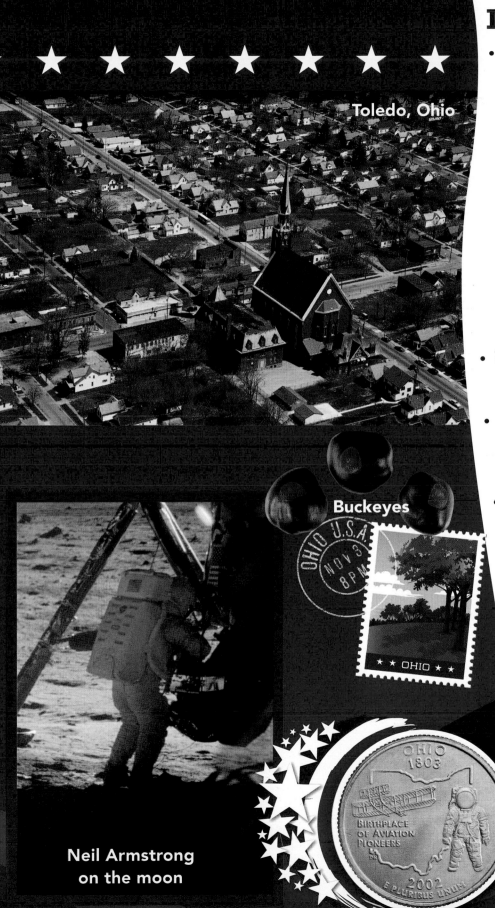

Toledo, Ohio

DID YOU KNOW?

- The very first hospital-based ambulance service was established in Cincinnati. It was Commercial Hospital, and the year was 1865.

An ambulance from 1895

- Cleveland is known for having America's first electric traffic light. It goes back to August 5, 1914.

- The first professional baseball team was the Cincinnati Red Stockings. They started in 1869.

- The first person to walk on the moon was Neil Armstrong. He was from Wapakoneta, Ohio.

Buckeyes

OHIO

Neil Armstrong on the moon

State flower: Red carnation

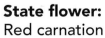

State bird: Cardinal

OKLAHOMA ★ ★ ★ ★ ★

STATE STATS

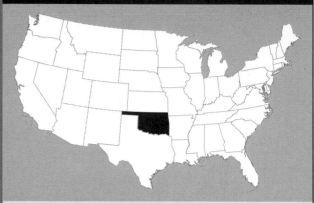

Square Miles: 69,899

Capital: Oklahoma City

Postal abbreviation: OK

U.S. region: The South

State motto: Labor conquers all things

OKLAHOMA

The blue of the flag background is meant to be like the banner carried by the Native American Choctaw people during the Civil War. The buffalo-skin shield is meant to be like that of an Osage warrior. What looks like six crosses are an American Indian design that stands for stars. There is also a peace pipe for Native Americans and an olive branch for peace for European Americans.

SPECIAL FOOD

Onion burgers

So good to have you here!

At 69,899 square miles, we are the 20th-largest state out of 50. Our state's name is directly connected to the native peoples here. It is from the native Choctaw language and connects the words "people," or "tribe," and "red." The capital is Oklahoma City, and it has one of the world's largest livestock markets. Come have a look around!

OKLAHOMA U.S.

OKLAHOMA ★ ★

Scissortail Bridge, Oklahoma City

Cherokee Pow wow

Tornadic supercell in the American plains near Oklahoma panhandle

DID YOU KNOW?

- In 1935, the world's first parking meter was installed on the southeast corner of what was then First Street and Robinson Avenue in Oklahoma City. It was known as Park-O-Meter No. 1.

- Opened in 1955, the National Cowboy & Western Heritage Museum is located in Oklahoma City. It has more than 28,000 Western and American Indian artworks and artifacts.

- The tribal capital of the Cherokee Nation is in Tahlequah (taw-LEE-kwah), Oklahoma. The Cherokee Nation is the largest tribe in the United States and has more than 370,000 citizens around the world.

State bird: Scissor-tailed flycatcher

State flower: Oklahoma rose

OREGON ★ ★ ★ ★ ★ ★ ★ ★ ★

STATE STATS

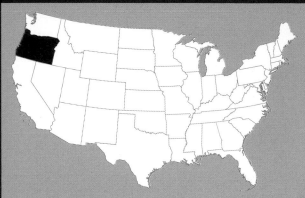

Square Miles: 98,379

Capital: Salem

Postal abbreviation: OR

U.S. region: The West

State motto: She flies with her own wings

The Oregon flag is unique among state flags because it has something different on both sides. The front side shows the state shield with the year Oregon became a state: 1859. The back of the flag shows the beaver, which is the state animal.

SPECIAL FOOD

Marionberry pie

Hi!

Welcome to the 9th-largest state! Though we believe our name is from a native language of this region, no one is really sure what it means. Long ago, Major Robert Rogers wrote the name in a petition to King George III. Salem, our capital, was a name that several wanted to use because it was a biblical name. It is a part of the name Jerusalem and means "peace." Hope you'll enjoy it here in Oregon!

★ OREGON ★

Oregon
942 FQL
4 16

Grapes in Willamette Valley

Sea Lion Caves

Mt. Hood

Heceta Head Lighthouse

DID YOU KNOW?

- The deepest lake in the United States is Crater Lake, at 1,946 feet. It is formed in what remains of an ancient volcano.

- The largest sea cave in the United States was discovered in 1880. If you go just north of Florence on the coast, you'll run across the entrance to Sea Lion Caves, which is 11 stories high and filled with very loud sea lions!

- One of the most photographed lighthouses in the world is on the Oregon coast. It's Heceta Head Lighthouse, which was built in 1894 and named after the Spanish explorer Bruno de Heceta.

- The caves now located in Oregon Caves National Monument were discovered in 1874. The solid marble was carved by water that flowed over them from the surface. Inside the cave is the River Styx, which happens to be the only subterranean river in the protected Wild Rivers System.

State bird:
Western Meadowlark

State flower:
Oregon grape

81

PENNSYLVANIA ★ ★ ★

STATE STATS

Square Miles: 46,054

Capital: Harrisburg

Postal abbreviation: PA

U.S. region: The Northeast

State motto: Virtue, liberty, and independence

The state's coat of arms is in the center of the blue background of the flag. The plow, the cornstalk, and the wheat stand for the state's abundant agriculture, the ship stands for the shipping commerce, and the olive branch stands for peace.

SPECIAL FOOD

Philly cheese steak

Nice to meet you!

The founder of our state was named William Penn, and an area here is named after his father, Admiral William Penn. Pennsylvania means "Penn's woods." Harrisburg, our capital city, has a long history. In 1719, a man named John Harris Sr. settled in the area and bought some land. His son, John Harris Jr., made plans for a town here in 1785 on his father's land and named it Harrisburg. We are now the 33rd largest of the 50 states. Welcome to Pennsylvania!

Rockville Bridge

PENNSYLVANIA NOV 3 3PM

★ PENNSYLVANIA ★

3-00 PENNSYLVANIA

AAD·0047

WWW.STATE.PA.US

Independence Hall, Philadelphia

Pittsburgh

DID YOU KNOW?

- The first circulatory library in America was started by Benjamin Franklin in Philadelphia in 1731.

- The longest stone masonry arch rail bridge in the world is Rockville Bridge in Harrisburg. It was finished in 1902, has 48 total arches, and is 3,820 feet long.

- The very first world series was played in 1903 between the Pittsburg Pirates and the Boston Americans. The first baseball stadium was built in 1909 in Pittsburg. It was named Forbes Field.

- The ENIAC or Electronic Numerical Integrator and Calculator was built by two University of Pennsylvania professors between 1943 and 1944. It is thought of as the grandfather of digital computers, even though it filled a 20-foot by 40-foot room!

State flower: Mountain laurel

State bird: Ruffed grouse

83

RHODE ISLAND ★ ★ ★

STATE STATS

Square Miles: 1,545

Capital: Providence

Postal abbreviation: RI

U.S. region: The Northeast

State motto: Hope

The state seal is gold in the center of the white flag. Just below an anchor is the word "Hope" on a ribbon. There are 13 golden stars surrounding the anchor that stand for the original 13 colonies, with Rhode Island as the 13th state.

SPECIAL FOOD

Coffee milk

Greetings!

Rhode Island is the smallest of the 50 states! We're not exactly sure, but we think our state's Greek name is a reference to the island of Rhodes that is in the Aegean Sea. We do know what our capital city's name means. In 1636, Roger Williams, who was a minister, named the area for "God's merciful Providence." This is God's guiding hand. May you find joy in God's providence here.

Providence, Rhode Island

DID YOU KNOW?

- Rhode Island isn't actually an island in itself, but it has land connected to other states, as well as 36 islands that are all a part of the state. It's the smallest of the states, while Alaska is the largest.

- The state was the last of the original 13 colonies to become a state.

- One of the nation's oldest carousels is the Flying Horse Carousel. It's located in the resort town of Watch Hill. Created in 1879, there are huge, hand-carved horses with leather saddles.

Flying Horse Carousel

- Rhode Island passed the first anti-slavery statute in the colonies. This was long ago, on May 18, 1652.

Block Island, Rhode Island

Historic Colourful Wooden House in Newport

State flower: Violet

State bird: Rhode Island Red

85

SOUTH CAROLINA ★

STATE STATS

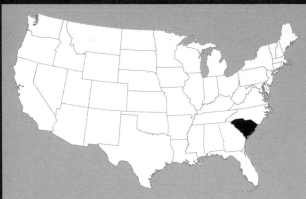

Square Miles: 32,020

Capital: Columbia

Postal abbreviation: SC

U.S. region: The South

State motto: Prepared in mind and resources/While I breathe, I hope

The troops from South Carolina wore a crescent moon on their hats when they fought in the Revolutionary War, and this symbol is in the upper left-hand corner of the flag. In the center of the flag is an image of the palmetto, the state's tree. The wood from the tree was so strong that British cannonballs just bounced off of it.

SPECIAL FOOD

Shrimp 'n' grits

Hello there!

Well, just like North Carolina, our state is named for King Charles I of England. And obviously, we are the Carolina on the south if you're looking at a map! Columbia, our capital city, was named in 1786. It's a name that stands for America since it is connected to Christopher Columbus. Out of the 50 states, we're ranked the 40th largest. Enjoy your stay!

Ravenel bridge

Victoria's harbour

Live Oak Tree Tunnel

DID YOU KNOW?

- Loggerhead sea turtles live on the coast, laying their eggs on the beaches. The babies hatch and make their way out to the ocean. Though their average weight is around 300 pounds, some grow as large as 1,000 pounds!

- The Francis Beidler Forest is considered the world's largest virgin Cyprus-tupelo swamp forest.

- The meat-eating Venus flytraps grow in North and South Carolina. They trap insects and spiders so they can eat them.

Young Loggerhead sea turtles

swamp forest

Smiling Faces. Beautiful Places.
325 AWK
4 South Carolina 99

State flower: Yellow Jessamine

State bird: Carolina wren

87

SOUTH DAKOTA ★ ★ ★

STATE STATS

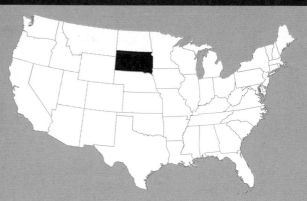

Square Miles: 77,116

Capital: Pierre

Postal abbreviation: SD

U.S. region: The Midwest

State motto: Under God, the people rule

South Dakota's state seal is in the center of the flag. On the seal, you can see a furnace, which stands for the state's mining, a farmer and plow, which stands for the state's agriculture, and beautiful scenes, which stand for the state's natural wonders. There is a golden sun around the seal, and circling the seal are the words "South Dakota, The Mount Rushmore State."

SPECIAL FOOD

Dessert lefse with butter & sugar

Hi!
So glad you could make it to South Dakota! You might have already guessed that we are just south of North Dakota, and our state name also means "ally" or "friend." A good name, for sure! We are the 17th-largest state at 77,116 square miles. Our capital city, Pierre, was named after Fort Pierre that was named after a fur trader from Missouri, Pierre Chouteau Jr. Have a look around!

South Dakota
4AA 656

Iron Creek Tunnel in Custer State Park

Mammoth Site

DID YOU KNOW?

- The third-longest cave in the world is Jewel Cave. There are more than 202 miles of passages that have been searched. The calcite crystals in the cave glitter when light hits them, and this gave the cave its name.

- What will be the world's largest sculpture is actually in progress in the Black Hills of Custer County. The Crazy Horse Memorial is going to be 563 feet high and 641 feet long. This memorial has an educational and cultural focus on the North American Indian. It's been under construction since 1948.

- The largest concentration of Columbian and woolly mammoth bones in the world have been discovered at Hot Springs in the area now called Mammoth Site.

Mt. Rushmore
National Memorial

American Bison —
South Dakota prairie

State flower:
American Pasque flower

State bird: Ring-necked pheasant

TENNESSEE ★ ★ ★ ★ ★

STATE STATS

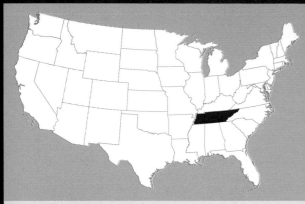

Square Miles: 42,144

Capital: Nashville

Postal abbreviation: TN

U.S. region: The South

State motto: Agriculture and commerce

In the center of the red Tennessee flag, you see a blue circle with three white stars, each star representing a different area of the state. One star stands for the western lowlands, one stands for the eastern mountains, and the final star stands for the farmland in between. The white ring surrounding the blue circle stands for the state's unbreakable unity.

SPECIAL FOOD

Nashville hot chicken sandwich

Here we are in Tennessee!

Our state's name is from the native Cherokee word *tanasi* that was used to describe a specific village, but we don't know what the name meant. We rank 36 out of the 50 states in size. Nashville is our capital city, and it was named in 1779 after General Francis Nash, who was in the American Revolutionary War. Welcome, friends!

Appalachian Mountains Viewed Along the Blue Ridge Parkway

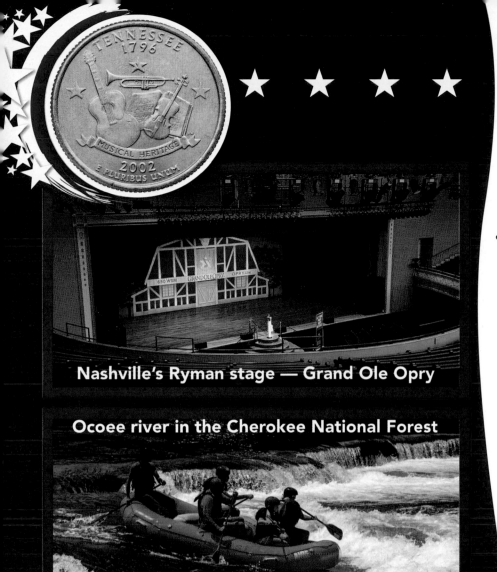

Nashville's Ryman stage — Grand Ole Opry

Ocoee river in the Cherokee National Forest

DID YOU KNOW?

- Nashville is considered the country music capital of the world. Country music began in the United States in the 1920s.

- Sequoyah, a native man born near Vonore, developed the Cherokee Indian alphabet. The alphabet had 86 syllables when first created in 1821 and helped the Cherokee people read and write their own language.

- The largest underground lake in the United States is in Craighead Caverns. Named the Lost Sea, it was discovered by a 13-year-old boy in 1905.

Lost Sea

- The first woman elected to the U.S. Senate was Hattie Caraway. She was born in Bakerville in 1878 and elected in 1932.

State flower: Iris

State bird: Mockingbird

TEXAS ★ ★ ★ ★ ★ ★ ★ ★ ★ ★ ★ ★ ★

STATE STATS

Square Miles: 268,596

Capital: Austin

Postal abbreviation: TX

U.S. region: The South

State motto: Friendship

The state flag of Texas has three simple stripes of red, white, and blue, with a single star in the center of the blue stripe. The color blue stands for loyalty, the color red for bravery, and the color white for strength and purity. The star reflects the nickname of Texas as the Lone Star State.

SPECIAL FOOD

Fajitas

Howdy!

Our state's name was originally from a native Caddo word that meant "friend." It was slightly changed in Spanish and was used to speak of the Caddo people. Austin, our capital, was named in 1839 for Stephen Austin, who is known as the "Father of Texas." Welcome to Texas, the second-largest state!

Texas State Capitol Building

TEXAS

BK6 ★ H598

The Lone Star State

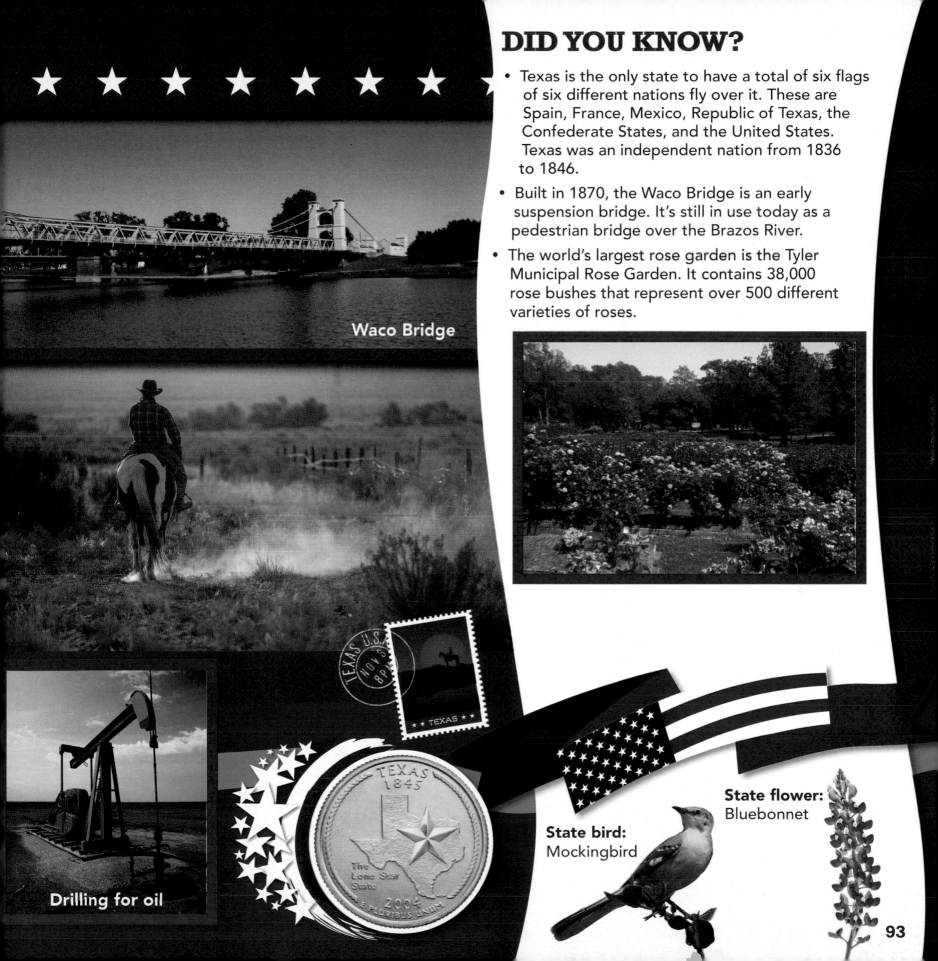

DID YOU KNOW?

- Texas is the only state to have a total of six flags of six different nations fly over it. These are Spain, France, Mexico, Republic of Texas, the Confederate States, and the United States. Texas was an independent nation from 1836 to 1846.

- Built in 1870, the Waco Bridge is an early suspension bridge. It's still in use today as a pedestrian bridge over the Brazos River.

- The world's largest rose garden is the Tyler Municipal Rose Garden. It contains 38,000 rose bushes that represent over 500 different varieties of roses.

Waco Bridge

Drilling for oil

TEXAS 1845
The Lone Star State
2004
E PLURIBUS UNUM

State bird:
Mockingbird

State flower:
Bluebonnet

93

UTAH ★ ★ ★ ★ ★ ★ ★ ★ ★ ★ ★ ★ ★

STATE STATS

Square Miles: 84,897

Capital: Salt Lake City

Postal abbreviation: UT

U.S. region: The West

State motto: Industry

There are several symbols on the Utah flag. These include an eagle holding two American flags, representing protection in times of war and peace, the date 1847, which is when the first Mormon settlers came here, and the date 1896, which is when Utah first became a state. The lily is the state flower and stands for peace, while the beehive stands for industry.

SPECIAL FOOD

Fry sauce

UTAH
V57 6AE
LIFE ELEVATED

Great Salt Lake

So happy to see you here in Utah!

The name of our state came from a native Apache word used to describe the Ute people. It means "people of the mountains." At 84,897 square miles, we're the 13th-largest state. Not far away from the capital is the Great Salt Lake, so the city was originally called Great Salt Lake City. We eventually dropped "Great" from the name. Enjoy your stay in Utah!

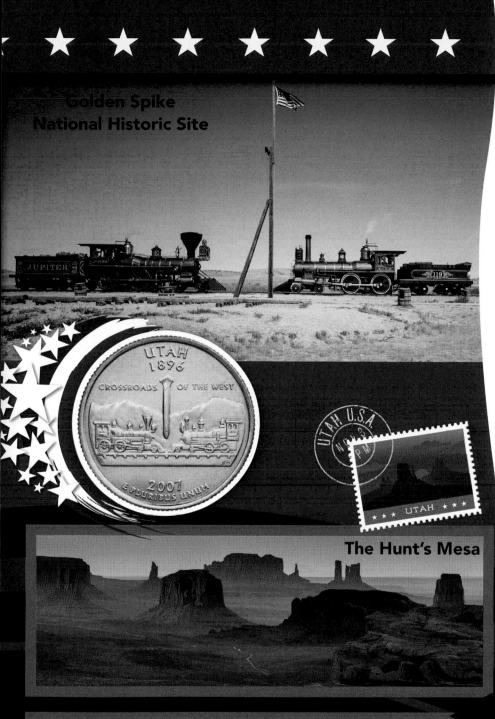

Golden Spike
National Historic Site

The Hunt's Mesa

Deer Valley

DID YOU KNOW?

- The completion of the world's first transcontinental railroad was celebrated here in Utah at Promontory Summit. It happened on May 10, 1869, where the Central Pacific and Union Pacific Railroads met. The place is now known as Golden Spike National Historic Site.

- At Rainbow Bridge National Monument, you'll see one of the world's largest natural rock spans, also considered the world's highest natural bridge. This wonder of God's world is a natural sculpture carved of solid sandstone that is 234 feet wide and 290 feet high.

- The town of Levan is simply "navel" spelled backward. It's thought to be named this because it's in the middle of the state.

State flower: Sego lily

State bird:
California gull

95

VERMONT ★ ★ ★ ★ ★ ★ ★ ★ ★

STATE STATS

Square Miles: 9,616

Capital: Montpelier

Postal abbreviation: VT

U.S. region: The Northeast

State motto: Freedom and unity

There are lots of images on Vermont's dark blue state flag that represent special things in the state. These include the deer that stands for wildlife, a pine tree that stands for their forests, wheat that stands for their agriculture, and a cow that stands for their dairy products.

SPECIAL FOOD

Apple cheddar pie

Hello!

Out of all the states, we rank 45th out of 50 in size, so we're pretty small. Our state's name is from a French phrase that means "green mountain." Montpelier became a town in 1781 and was named after a French city by that name. Now it's our capital. Thanks for coming to Vermont!

Montpelier, Vermont

Vermont

CGX 308

Green Mountain State   SEP

DID YOU KNOW?

- Vermont produces more maple syrup than any other state. The Vermont Maple Sugar Maker's Association was founded in 1893.

- Maria Vonn Trapp came with her family to Vermont after escaping the Nazis in Europe. It was their story that inspired *The Sound of Music*. Once in Vermont, she opened a ski lodge in Stowe. Her book, *Yesterday, Today, and Forever*, tells the story of how she and her husband taught their children about the life of Jesus. It came out in 1975 and was the first book published by the company that designed this book you're reading now!

- The smallest state capital in the U.S. is Montpelier, Vermont, with a population of fewer than 8,000 people.

Large maple tree with sap buckets

Old-fashioned covered bridge

State flower: Red clover

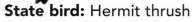

State bird: Hermit thrush

VIRGINIA ★ ★ ★ ★ ★ ★ ★ ★

STATE STATS

Square Miles: 42,775

Capital: Richmond

Postal abbreviation: VA

U.S. region: The South

State motto: Thus always to tyrants

On the blue state flag is the state seal in white with the motto in Latin, *sic semper tyrannis*, which means "Thus always to tyrants." The picture of the female warrior standing over the defeated king shows his crown knocked off and relates clearly to the words. The warrior is Virtue, which represents Virginia, and the tyrant stands for Great Britain.

SPECIAL FOOD

Brunswick Stew

How is your day?

Hope you're doing really well! Our state's name is in honor of Elizabeth I of England. She was known as the "virgin queen" because she never got married. Out of the 50 states, we rank 35th in size at 42,775 square miles. Our capital city reminded someone of a place in England that looked similar, so he named the area Richmond, too. Now it is time to explore!

Richmond, Virginia

VIRGINIA
VA4LVRS
VIRGINIA IS FOR LOVERS
Virginia.org

DID YOU KNOW?

- The first permanent English settlement in America was Jamestown, founded in 1607. This was also the first capital of Virginia.

- Considered the world's largest living history museum, Colonial Williamsburg is a place that recreates an 18th-century city. You can find food, crafts, and reenactments from that period to experience.

- Wild ponies have roamed free on Assateague Island since the 1600s. Some think they arrived here when a Spanish ship with lots of horses was wrecked offshore. Part of this island is here in Virginia and part of it is in Maryland.

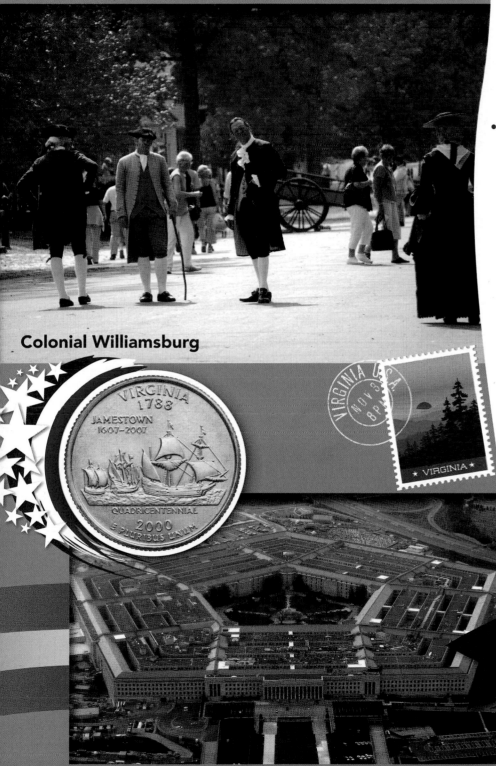

Colonial Williamsburg

- There was an actual day marked as a day of thanksgiving that happened at Berkeley Hundred in Virginia in 1619. This was two years before the Pilgrims celebrated their Thanksgiving.

The Department of Defense is in Arlington at the Pentagon, the world's largest office building.

State flower: Flowering dogwood

State bird: Cardinal

WASHINGTON ★ ★ ★ ★

STATE STATS

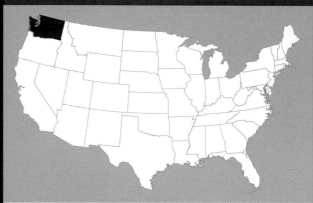

Square Miles: 71,298

Capital: Olympia

Postal abbreviation: WA

U.S. region: The West

State motto: By and by

In the center of the deep green flag is the state seal, which shows George Washington, the first president and the one whom the state is named after; 1889 is the year that Washington officially became a state.

SPECIAL FOOD

Salmon

So good of you to come!

Our state is named after George Washington, the first president of the United States. We are the 18th-largest state. Our capital city, Olympia, was named in 1850. Because it had a good view of the Olympic Mountains, they thought the name Olympia seemed good. Have a good time here in Washington!

WASHINGTON
AZM9590
EVERGREEN STATE

Mount Rainier Sunset Over Olympia, Washington

Hoh Rain Forest

North Head Lighthouse

Space Needle, Seattle

DID YOU KNOW?

- More than 140 inches of rain falls in the Hoh Rain Forest in Olympic National Park every year.
- The state of Washington is the only state to be named after a United States president.

Boeing factory

- Everett is the site of the world's largest building by total volume. This is the Boeing factory building, which is 4,280,000 square feet.

State Amphibian: Pacific chorus frog

State flower: Rhododendron

State bird: American goldfinch

WASHINGTON 1889 · THE EVERGREEN STATE · 2007 · E PLURIBUS UNUM

101

WEST VIRGINIA ★ ★ ★

STATE STATS

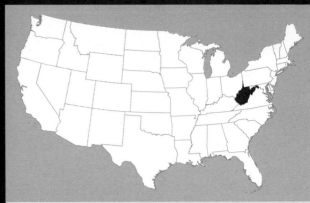

Square Miles: 24,230

Capital: Charleston

Postal abbreviation: WV

U.S. region: The South

State motto: Mountaineers are always free

The flag has a white background with blue trim. The date of June 20, 1863 is on the flag, which is when West Virginia became a state. One of the men on the flag stands for mining, and one stands for agriculture.

SPECIAL FOOD

Pepperoni rolls

Hi friends!

Like Virginia, we're named after Elizabeth I of England. Our states separated during the Civil War. At 24,230 square miles, we rank as the 41st-largest state. Charleston, our capital, was named after Colonel George Clendenin's father, Charles, and was originally just Charles Town. Glad to see you here in West Virginia!

WEST VIRGINIA
NOV 3 3PM

★ WEST VIRGINIA ★

WEST VIRGINIA
1863
NEW RIVER GORGE
2005
E PLURIBUS UNUM

Charleston

West Virginia
ABC 999
Wild, Wonderful

New River Gorge

DID YOU KNOW?

- A special variety of the yellow apple, what we call a Golden Delicious, originated in Clay County in the late 1800s. The original Grimes Golden Apple Tree was discovered in Wellsburg in 1832.

GRIMES GOLDEN (1921-089)

- The first observation of Mother's Day was on May 10, 1908. This was done at Andrew's Methodist Church in Grafton. The purpose of the ceremony was a memorial for the mother of Anna Jarvis.

- West Virginia became a state in 1863, at the beginning of the Civil War. In fact, it is the only state to be formed by separating from a Confederate state.

State flower: Rhododendron

State bird: Northern Cardinal

103

STATE STATS

Square Miles: 65,496

Capital: Madison

Postal abbreviation: WI

U.S. region: The Midwest

State motto: Forward

WISCONSIN
1848

On the flag, there is a sailor, representing the importance of water, and a miner, representing the importance of working the land. The shield has symbols that stand for mining, agriculture, navigation, and manufacturing. On the bottom, you can see a pyramid made of triangles that stand for bars of iron. These bars are called ingots, and these ingots stand for the 13 original states.

SPECIAL FOOD ▸ **Fried cheese curds**

So nice to have you here!

The name of our state is from a native Miami word that can mean "it lies red" or "river running through a red place," referring to the Wisconsin River. We rank 23rd out of the 50 states in size. Madison, our capital, was named after the fourth president, James Madison. It's interesting that the first streets were named after the 39 signers of the U.S. Constitution. Come look around the state!

WISCONSIN
777-LLL
JUN • America's Dairyland • 07

Madison, Wisconsin

Wisconsin dairy farm

Sugar Loaf Island, Part of the Wisconsin Dells

DID YOU KNOW?

- You can find the world's largest carousel at the House on the Rock in Spring Green. It has an amazing 269 different carousel animals and 20,000 lights.

- The first hydroelectric plant in the United States was built at Fox River in Appleton in 1882. It was called the Vulcan Street Plant.

Appleton Locks & Dams, Fox River

- Wisconsin grows more cranberries than any other state. They grow in bogs or boglands, which are very wet areas, and this makes it easier to harvest since cranberries float.

Wisconsin cranberry marsh

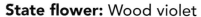

State flower: Wood violet

State bird: American Robin

105

WYOMING ★ ★ ★ ★ ★ ★ ★

STATE STATS

Square Miles: 97,813

Capital: Cheyenne

Postal abbreviation: WY

U.S. region: The West

State motto: Equal rights

This flag was designed by a woman by the name of Verna Keays, who designed it for a state contest. The state seal is shown on a silhouette of a bison, the state animal. The men on the shield stand for miners and ranchers. The red in the flag symbolizes both the native peoples and the blood of the pioneers, while the white stands for purity, and the blue stands for both the sky and for justice.

SPECIAL FOOD

Buffalo jerky

Howdy!

We're the tenth-largest state! Our state's name is from a native word that means "at the big river flat" or possibly "mountains and valleys alternating." Our capital city was named after the American Indian tribe so significant in this area, the Cheyenne. So glad you made it here to Wyoming!

Cheyenne, Wyoming

17 53194
WYOMING

Devils Tower

DID YOU KNOW?

- Yellowstone became the first official national park in 1872. Devils Tower became the first national monument in 1906. Both are here!

- While you might know that Wyoming's license plates feature a man on a bucking bronco, did you know that the horse has a name? It is named after a bronc that could not be ridden long ago: "Old Steamboat."

- Wolves that were once endangered were reintroduced into Wyoming. Now those wolves thrive here.

State flower: Wyoming Indian paintbrush

State bird: Western meadowlark

WASHINGTON, D.C.

CAPITAL STATS

Square Miles: 68 square miles

Capital of United States: Nationhood — July 4, 1776

Postal abbreviation: DC

U.S. region: The South

Nation's motto: In God we trust

The flag of Washington, D.C., is based on George Washington's coat of arms.

National Anthem: "The Star-Spangled Banner" (adopted 1931)

Name: Washington in honor of the first president. District of Columbia in honor of Christopher Columbus.

Washington Monument

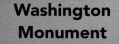

WASHINGTON, DC
FN ★★★ 9713
END TAXATION WITHOUT REPRESENTATION

Welcome to our nation's capital!

Leaders from every state come here to help guide the nation.

White House

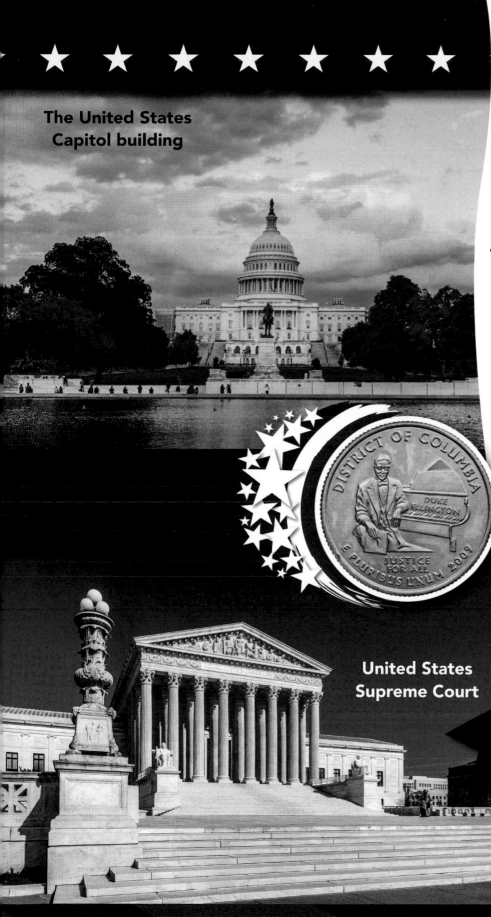

The United States Capitol building

United States Supreme Court

DID YOU KNOW?

- Before Washington, D.C. became the capital of the United States, the leaders of the government had met in several cities, including Philadelphia, Pennsylvania, New York, New York, and Princeton, New Jersey.

- The area that would become the permanent capital city was actually chosen by President George Washington, after Congress authorized him to choose a site along the banks of the Potomac River.

- The total area of land set aside for Washington, D.C. was not to exceed 100 square miles. It was proposed that land be purchased for $66.66 an acre if public buildings were to be built on it, while land for roadways would be given up for free.

- President Washington recommended that Pierre Charles L'Enfant, a French major who stayed behind after the war, should draw up plans for the capital. In just a few months, he had developed a design for the city and its streets, based in part on cities of Europe like Paris and Milan, as well as like Williamsburg, the capital of Virginia.

- What we now call the White House, where the president lives, was originally called the Presidential Palace. James Hoban created the first design for a $500 prize, taking inspiration from the Irish country houses of his youth. President John Adams moved in on November 1, 1800 during his last year as president.

Official flower: American Beauty rose

Official bird: Wood thrush

FLAGS ★ ★ ★ ★ ★ ★ ★ ★ ★

Name that flag: Take a few moments to describe the colors and images on a flag and see if anyone can figure out the state.

OKLAHOMA

STATE OF OREGON

1859

SOUTH DAKOTA

WISCONSIN

1848

**Flag of the United States
(1777-1795)**

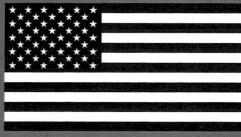

Flag of the United States

? Did you really know: Read different statements from the Did You Know? section of the book and see if people can guess the state.

✝ Prayer for the states: Take a few moments each day to look up a state and pray for the people there. You might watch the national news or look up recent news stories to determine where the greatest needs are.

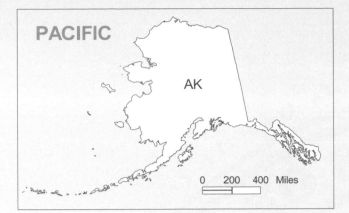

PACIFIC

AK

0   200   400   Miles

WEST

WA

OR

PACIFIC

MT

ID

WY

N

SD

NV

MOUNTAIN

CA

UT

CO

AZ

NM

0   200   400   Miles

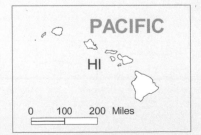

PACIFIC

HI

0   100   200   Miles